DESERT DANGER

JIM E...

To Lynne, with love

While the events described and some of the characters in this book may
be based on actual historical events and real people, Tim Jackson
is a fictional character, created by the author, and his story
is a work of fiction.

Scholastic Children's Books
Commonwealth House, 1–19 New Oxford Street,
London, WC1A 1NU, UK
A division of Scholastic Ltd
London ~ New York ~ Toronto ~ Sydney ~ Auckland
Mexico City ~ New Delhi ~ Hong Kong

Published in the UK by Scholastic Ltd, 2005
This edition published 2013

ISBN 978 1407 13669 1

Printed and bound in the UK by CPI Group (UK) Ltd, Croydon, CR0 4YY

2 4 6 8 10 9 7 5 3 1

I was trying to mend the clutch on a police car in my Uncle George's garage, when the bomb went off. One minute I was in the pit under the car, looking at the frayed clutch cable, the next … BOOOOOOMM!!! … there was an almighty explosion from a few streets away and the garage shook as though it had been hit by an earthquake. My first thought was that the brick roof of the arch was going to come down on top of me; I heard my uncle shouting, "Tim! Get out of there quick!" and I knew he thought so too.

I leapt rather than climbed up the ladder out of the pit and ran for the entrance to the arch, my hands over my head in the hope I'd be able to ward off any bricks if they fell down on me. Uncle George's garage was inside one of the arches at the back of St Pancras railway station, in the centre of London, not far from King's Cross. The arches were like small tunnels that had been built under the railway line, brick caves about 100 feet deep. Small businesses rented out these arches. Some were motor repairers, like Uncle George. There was an electrician, a plumber, and a bloke who sold second-hand furniture – all sorts of businesses. So far the arches had stood up well to the bombing that had been going on since the War started more than two years before; none of them had caved in – yet. But, now that the Germans were dropping bombs on London, and especially as we were so near three of London's biggest railway stations, St Pancras, King's Cross and Euston, our area had become a major target. I think all of us who worked there felt that sooner or later the Germans would score a direct hit on the arches – and then it would be the end for all of us.

I stood in the street next to Uncle George and looked towards Euston. A big cloud of smoke was billowing up from one of the streets near the station.

"I didn't hear any sirens," I said, bewildered. Usually, when there was an air-raid, the sirens went off to tell you the bombers were coming, and you usually had time to get to the nearest air-raid shelter.

"There weren't any," replied Uncle George. "I bet you it was an unexploded bomb from an earlier raid, just sitting there waiting for something to set it off."

That happened sometimes: a bomb would be dropped from the German planes and not go off. Sometimes they'd be buried deep in the ground, and then they'd just sit there, hidden, until one day something would trigger the explosion – a vibration, or something – and the bomb would blow up, destroying everything around it.

"I'd better get over there and see if I can do anything to help," said Uncle George hurriedly.

"I'm coming with you," I told him.

"No," said Uncle George firmly. "There could be anything going on there: a leaking gas main, fires, buildings collapsing. Your mother would have my guts for garters if anything happened to you."

My mother was Uncle George's sister. It was funny really, Uncle George was over six feet tall and built like a shed on legs, with a broken nose from the time when he'd been a boxer, and yet he was scared stiff of Mum, who was small and thin. I suppose it was because Mum had a bit of a tongue on her and didn't hold back when she felt like using it.

Me, I'm Tim Jackson, eighteen years old. My eighteenth birthday had been the week before, on 27 March 1942. I was waiting for my papers to arrive at any time, calling me up into the Army to go off and fight.

"But I'll be going into the Army any day now, Uncle George," I protested. "Anything could happen to me once I go, so I might as well come with you now."

"No," repeated Uncle George firmly. "For one thing, I'm trained to deal with this – you're not. Also, if you go off to war and get killed or injured, that'll be Adolf Hitler's fault. If you go with me now and something happens to you, it'll be my fault. Your mum's not likely to have a go at Hitler, but sure as eggs is eggs she'd have a go at me. You stay here and get on with that clutch. It ain't going to be mended on its own, and that vehicle is needed for vital war work."

"OK, Uncle," I said resignedly.

Uncle George grabbed his bag, which held his gas mask and some tools, and set off towards Euston. With all the bombing that had gone on, lots of the roads had great big holes in them, or were blocked by rubble from collapsed buildings, so if you were going somewhere relatively close by, it was usually quicker on foot than by car.

When Uncle George talked about being "trained to deal with this", he meant that he was an official Civil Defence Warden. He'd wanted to go to war himself, but the War Office told him that as a car mechanic he was in a "reserved occupation". This meant that they needed him to stay at home in England and help keep things on the move. Someone had to keep the fire engines and police cars on the road, so he stayed behind and worked on the vehicles. He also did his bit as a volunteer Civil Defence Warden, going out on emergency calls as an auxiliary fireman, and digging victims out of collapsed buildings after bombing raids. I was his apprentice, learning to be a motor mechanic. I'd been with him for the past four years, since I'd left school at the age of fourteen.

I went back into the tunnel and climbed down into the pit, then I set to work on the clutch of a police car. Most of the vehicles we had coming into the garage were official: police cars, ambulances, fire engines. Because of petrol rationing, very few people could run a car of their own.

Most of the vehicles we had in were also pretty badly beaten up from being driven along streets carved up by bombs. London had been especially hard hit in the last two and a half years since the War began. Eighteen months before, during the Blitz, the Germans bombed London every night throughout September and October. It wasn't only London, nearly every other major city in Britain was bombed, but London, being the capital, took the brunt of it. Mrs Jepson, who lived next door to us, told us that Coventry city centre had been completely destroyed in a series of bombing raids in November 1940. She knew because she had a daughter who lived in Birmingham. All I knew about were the raids on London. They reckoned well over one million homes were destroyed, and about 15,000 Londoners were killed in the Blitz. It often struck me and my family that we were lucky to be alive. Everyone knew of people who'd been killed, or had their homes flattened. Every time the bombers came over it was a game of chance: would we be alive in the morning, or would it be our turn to die?

Although some people said the bombing wasn't as bad as it had been in 1940, it seemed even worse to me. Most nights the big German bombers still came over, the air-raid sirens wailed, and we all hurried down into the underground stations that doubled as huge air-raid shelters. Some people actually lived in the underground stations, they even had beds and tables and chairs set up on the platforms. I couldn't stand being in the air-raid shelter. I would just sit there and wait for the All Clear to sound so I could get up to street level again, back to the fresh air. Although when we did come up the air was rarely fresh – it usually smelt of burning.

I think everyone believed things would get better when the Americans had joined the War five months before, in December 1941. Uncle George certainly did. I remember him and Mum talking in our kitchen after they'd heard the news on the wireless.

"You see, Ada, now the Americans have come in, this war will soon be over," he told her, with a big grin on his face. "I give it two months before Hitler surrenders."

"Oh, do you?" Mum had snapped back. "And when did you become an expert on the War, George Wilson?"

"Well, it's obvious, ain't it?" said Uncle George. "The Americans have got all the best weapons. They'll slaughter the Germans."

"The Americans only came into this war because Japan bombed their navy," said my mother. "As far as they're concerned this war is about them against the Japanese. Half of America is German, anyway. Why should they support us against Hitler?"

"Because…" began Uncle George, but Mum just gave one of her sniffs and that shut him up.

Like I say, that had been five months ago, and Germany still showed no signs of surrendering. There were those who reckoned the Americans had joined us too late anyway, that we'd already lost the War. With the Germans seeming to get stronger, and the Japanese defeating our armies in Malaya and Singapore, a lot of people thought Hitler would be in London by June. But if anybody said anything like that when Mum was around, she got really mad.

"No way is that squirt Hitler going to set foot in this country," she'd say angrily. "We beat his lot in 1918, and we'll beat 'em again this time round."

I was just putting the finishing touches to the clutch on the police car, when Uncle George came back. As I climbed out of the pit, I could tell by the unhappy expression on his face that it had been difficult.

"Anything bad, Uncle George?" I asked.

He nodded. "Two kids," he said. "Boy and a girl, aged six and seven. Brother and sister. They shouldn't have been out on their own."

"What happened?" I asked.

He sighed, miserably. "They must have been playing and found the bomb poking out of the ground. No one knows for sure what happened, but they must have set it off. Both of 'em blown to bits. Their mum only knew it was them when I found their shoes." He shook his head. "I hate this war," he sighed. "How's that clutch coming along?"

"All fixed," I said.

"Good," he replied. "Let's close up here and go home."

We shut the gates of the repair shop and Uncle George locked up, and then we began to walk home. It wasn't far, only a mile.

As we walked, I asked him: "Uncle George, do you reckon we're going to win this war?"

"Of course we are," he said, surprised. "What makes you even ask?"

"Sometimes I hear the ambulance drivers talking, or one of the fire crews, while I'm fixing one of their vehicles, and all they talk about is how many more buildings have been destroyed, and how many people have been killed. I sometimes wonder if we can last."

"'Course we can," he said defiantly. "We beat 'em last time around and we'll beat 'em again this time."

"You sound just like Mum," I laughed. "That's what she says."

"Well, your mother knows best, Tim," he said.

We walked along Crowndale Road and then up Royal College Street in silence. I could tell from the expression on Uncle George's face that he was thinking about the children whose shoes he had just found. I wondered whether I should start talking to him about something else to take his mind off it, but then I decided it was best to say nothing.

Finally we came to the turning for Plender Street. Uncle George lived six houses further up Royal College Street; Mum and I lived at Selous Mews.

"See you in the morning, Tim," he said. "Unless there's an air-raid, in which case I'll see you in the shelter. Keep an eye on your mum."

"I will, Uncle," I assured him.

Mum was in the kitchen when I got home, boiling a saucepan of hot water on the gas stove so she could do the washing. It was one of the things she was keen on – making sure the two of us had clean clothes. Nearly every day she put dirty clothes to soak in an old bucket in the yard, and then, when most of the dirt had come out, she put a big saucepan on the stove and boiled the clothes clean. I'd come home filthy from Uncle George's garage, so there was a saucepan of water boiling up clean clothes for me every other day.

I'm an only child. My father had been killed in an accident just before I was born, so I never knew him. Mum didn't have any photographs of him, either, so I never found out what he looked like. I guess he looked just like me, because every now and then Mum would look at me and say, "You look just like your father!" I was never sure whether that was a good thing or a bad thing. I don't know why Mum never married again. Uncle George said it was because most men don't want to take on another man's kid, referring to me. Personally, I think the real reason is that Mum's got a very sharp tongue, and she'd scare the life out of most men.

"How was your day, Tim?" she asked.

"All right," I said. "A bomb went off over near Euston. Uncle George went over to deal with it."

Mum lowered the gas under the boiling saucepan, and then asked, "Was he all right?"

"Yeah," I said. "He was upset, though. Two kids got killed."

Mum shook her head and her face tightened in anger. The death of a child always upset her. She said to me once, "Parents should never have to bury their kids. It's not natural."

"A letter came for you," she said. "I put it by the clock on the mantelpiece."

I went over to the fireplace and when I saw the official-looking brown envelope, my heart gave a leap. I hoped this was my call-up papers! I was desperate to get overseas and into the War, to fight for my country and give Hitler a bloody nose.

I opened the envelope excitedly. It was an official letter telling me to report to Number 1 Training Battalion, Royal Engineers, at Napier Barracks, Shorncliffe, Kent on 11 April. Enclosed with the letter was a railway travel warrant, and details of how to get to Shorncliffe. I was to catch the Folkestone train from London Bridge and get off at Cheriton, which was the nearest railway station.

"I've been called up, Mum," I said. "I go for training next week."

Mum simply nodded. She was never one for showing her emotions. "You'll need clean clothes, then," she said.

After we'd had our supper, I sat and read the paper while Mum got out her knitting needles. She was making woolly hats for soldiers. It was part of a scheme the Government had set up, or the Women's Voluntary Service, or some such organization. It struck me that soldiers didn't need woolly hats as much as they needed steel helmets, but I didn't like to tell her so, because it would only upset her. Knitting gave her something to do, especially as she couldn't read, so couldn't pass the time reading a newspaper or a book or anything. I remember how surprised I was when I found out that she couldn't read or write. Mum was angry at my reaction.

"We never had education when we were kids," she told me sharply.

"But Uncle George can read and write," I pointed out.

"That's different," she explained. "He was a boy. Boys got education. Girls didn't."

I didn't think that was strictly true, because I knew lots of women who lived near us who could read and write, but I didn't like to argue with Mum. It didn't pay to argue with her if I wanted a quiet life.

We were sitting there in the kitchen, reading and knitting, when suddenly the air-raid siren screamed. I always hated that sound, even though it saved our lives time and time again. It was a high-pitched whine and it went right through you as it got louder and louder. Mum and I were well practised. We grabbed our coats and gas masks, and rushed out of the front door towards Mornington Crescent tube station, the nearest one to us. All our neighbours were doing the same. Everyone was fully dressed. In these uncertain days, with the threat of an air-raid nearly every night, everyone went to bed with their clothes on, just in case they had to run for cover. Some people even slept with their shoes on, to save them time in case the siren went off.

Usually we had about fifteen minutes from the time the siren sounded to get to the underground station before the bombs fell. It isn't a very long time, especially when you're thinking of those bombers on their way.

We were running along, when Mum suddenly tripped and fell. Luckily I managed to catch hold of her just before she hit the ground. As I held her, I was surprised how light she was. I'd always known she was thin, but I hadn't realized how little of her there was.

"You all right, Mum?" I asked.

"'Course I am," she snapped. "It's these shoes I'm wearing. The buckle's gone on the left one."

"Well you can't run in it," I said. "I'll carry you."

As I went to lift her up, she belted me with her gas mask.

"Get off me!" she ordered. "I ain't being carried anywhere. I'm perfectly capable of getting to the shelter under my own steam."

With that, she took off both her shoes, and then, holding her shoes and her gas mask, she started to run again in her stockinged feet. I ran beside her, watching out in case she fell over again, but we made it to the station with no further problems.

"Hurry up!" shouted the Air-raid Warden who was on duty beside the entrance. "The Germans are coming!" Then he saw that Mum hadn't got her shoes on, and asked: "What's happened to your shoes, love?"

"I'm saving 'em to look nice when I meet the King," she snapped back.

She and I hurried down the stairs towards the platforms. As we did, we met Uncle George, who was hurrying up the stairs the other way.

"There you are!" he exclaimed. "I was worried. I was just coming to find you."

"Mum's shoe went funny on her," I said. "The buckle bust."

"I can talk for myself, thank you very much, Tim Jackson," said Mum sharply. To Uncle George, she said: "Is Ivy here?"

Ivy was George's wife.

"Yes," nodded Uncle George. "She's saving a spot for us on the platform."

"Right," said Mum. "Let's find her. She might have a needle and thread and I can sew this buckle back on."

The three of us hurried down to the platform together, and as we got there I saw a couple of my old school pals, Denny Brown and Chaz Watson, sitting down playing cards. They waved at me to come and join them.

"There's Denny and Chaz," I told my mum. "I'm just going to tell them about getting my call-up papers."

"Your call-up papers?" echoed Uncle George. "When do you go?"

"Next week," I said.

"That's a bit soon," muttered Uncle George, unhappily.

"Not soon enough for Tim," said Mum. "He can't wait to get away." She looked towards Denny and Chaz, and then said to me, "No playing cards with that pair. They'll take your money off you."

"I haven't got any money," I pointed out. "I give all my wages to you."

"Lucky for you I look after 'em," said Mum. "Go on, then. And don't get into trouble."

As Mum and Uncle George went off to look for Aunt Ivy, I went over to Denny and Chaz. They were both grinning broadly.

"Me and Chaz have been called up!" said Denny, and he produced a brown envelope just like the one I'd got.

"Yeah. We're going into the infantry," said Chaz.

"I've been called up, too," I told them. "Royal Engineers. I report for training next Wednesday."

"Me and Chaz go on Monday," grinned Denny. "So we'll be ahead of you, Tim boy! We'll be out there sorting the Jerries out!"

At that moment there was the sound of a huge thud

that shook the whole station. Everyone fell silent and instinctively we all looked up at the curved roof above us, looking for any cracks.

"That was a close one," murmured Denny.

"I wonder if our house is still standing," muttered Chaz.

It was the question we all asked ourselves, every time we came down to the underground and listened to the bombs falling outside, feeling the vibration as the walls and roof of the station shook around us. Had our houses been hit? What would we find when we came out of the shelter? Had anyone we knew been killed?

The bombing raid went on for two hours. The whole time, the tube station shook as the bombs struck, but being deep underground, it held.

Finally, after what seemed like an age, the All Clear sounded, and we clambered up the winding staircase to the street. Mum had spent the whole time sewing the buckle back on her shoe, so she could walk normally.

When we stepped outside, the first thing that hit me – as always – was the smell of burning rubber. Whatever got hit, it was always the rubber from things like tyres that had the strongest smell. In the darkness, fires raged and piles of rubble lay where buildings had once stood. The fire engines were already at work, trying to put out the biggest fires, the fire-fighters silhouetted against the red and yellow lights from the flickering flames. Sparks blew about in the air.

I put my handkerchief over my mouth and nose to keep the choking black smoke out of my lungs. In front of me, London burned.

I had one more week of this, and then I'd be away, fighting to put a stop to it.

11 April 1942

One week later I was on my way. I packed my bags, said goodbye to Uncle George and Aunt Ivy, and the mates of mine who were still waiting to be called up, and went off to fight Hitler.

Mum came with me to London Bridge station, where I was catching the train to Cheriton. There were a few other blokes standing around at the station, and I guessed they were waiting for the same train. I felt a bit embarrassed, standing there with my mother; it made me feel like a little kid. "I'll be all right on my own now, Mum," I said, trying to be tactful.

Mum looked around at the other young men and nodded.

"Yeah, 'course you will," she said. "But make sure you write and let me know how you're getting on. I'll get your Uncle George to read it to me."

"I'll write as soon as I can," I told her.

She hesitated, then stood on her tiptoes and gave me a quick kiss on the cheek. "Come back alive, son," she whispered. Then she turned and walked away. As I watched her go I felt guilty for making her leave. She was going to miss me a lot – I was all she had.

A tall, thin young chap with ginger hair came over and joined me, and sighed as he watched my mum walk out of the station.

"Mothers, eh?" he said. "Mine wanted to come and see me off, but I begged her not to. She'd only have made a scene – lots of crying. She means well, but I'd never have lived it down." He held out his hand. "The name's Steve Matthews, but everyone calls me Ginger."

I shook his hand. "Tim Jackson," I said. "Are you off to Shorncliffe?"

Ginger nodded. "That's right," he said. "Royal Engineers."

"Me, too," I told him.

There was a yell from a station attendant: "Folkestone train from platform seven!", and suddenly the station was full of blokes, all about my age, all heading for platform seven.

"Where did they all come from?" asked Ginger, stunned.

"They must have been hanging about in the cafeteria, or something," I said. "Come on, we'd better get a move on or we won't get a seat, and I bet it's a long journey to Cheriton."

Ginger and I broke into a run, pushing our way through the crowd. A few of the men gave us annoyed looks as we ran past them, but it was lucky we did. There weren't enough seats for all us, let alone the ordinary civilians who were catching the same train to Folkestone.

Ginger and I managed to grab the last two seats in one of the eight-seater compartments. The six people who were already in it included a couple of elderly ladies, a middle-aged man and woman, and two men of our age.

"Heading for Shorncliffe?" I asked them.

The middle-aged man and woman and the two elderly ladies ignored me. In fact the middle-aged man gave a disapproving sniff and started reading a newspaper.

The two young blokes nodded.

"I'm Pete Morgan," one of them introduced himself. He was short and tubby, with black hair cropped close at the sides, but sticking up on the top of his head like a carpet. He had a thick Welsh accent.

"I'm Edward White," said the other. He was also shortish, with a mop of blond hair that hung down over his forehead. He added: "Everyone calls me Chalky."

He had a strange accent, which made it difficult to work out what he was saying. It was almost foreign.

"Tim Jackson," I said, pointing to myself.

"Ginger Matthews," Ginger introduced himself. "Have you come far?"

"Cardiff," said Pete.

"Cor, that's a long way!" exclaimed Ginger.

"I haven't come as far as him," said Pete, jerking his thumb at Chalky. "He's come all the way from Newcastle."

Newcastle, right up almost to Scotland. That explained Chalky's strange accent. My Uncle George called them Geordies.

"Newcastle?" I echoed. "Haven't they got any training camps up there?"

"They had one, but it got bombed," Chalky explained. "So that's why I've been sent down here."

"Can't you fellows read?" snapped the middle-aged man angrily.

We all looked at him blankly, and then at one another.

"Why, do you want help reading your newspaper?" asked Ginger cheekily.

The man scowled and pointed a finger at a notice just below the luggage racks. It was a cartoon of two people talking, with Adolf Hitler hiding behind a wooden crate, listening to them. The slogan read "Careless talk costs lives".

"Careless talk costs lives," announced the man firmly, just in case we couldn't read.

"But I'm not talking carelessly," protested Chalky. "I'm just saying why I had to come all this way to join up."

"You have revealed that your training camp has been bombed," snapped the man, obviously very annoyed. "That's the sort of information that would be useful to the enemy."

"Well as it was the enemy that bombed it, I expect they already know about it," retorted Ginger.

"Are you being cheeky?" demanded the man.

"No, I'm being sensible," replied Ginger.

"Don't talk to them, Eric," said his wife. "They're just hooligans out looking for trouble."

"Hooligans?" I echoed indignantly. "We're on our way to fight for our country, missus."

"Don't you talk to my wife that way, you hooligan!" snapped the man. "And don't you think you can get tough with me, either. I fought in the last war!"

"And he was wounded!" added his wife.

I was going to make a crack back at him, but I caught Chalky's eye and he shook his head, as if to say "Leave it alone. We don't want any trouble." I shut up.

That's the trouble with old folk – they see a bunch of young guys together and automatically think we're out for trouble. And they always think that we're never as good as they were when they were young.

We spent the rest of the journey in an unhappy silence, staring out of the window, watching the landscape and towns go by. Now and then one of us would start to say something, but then Eric the Miserable would glare at us as if we were committing treason and we'd shut up. I was glad when the train finally pulled in at Cheriton.

There was a row of single-decker buses waiting for us outside the station, each one with a piece of paper stuck on the driver's window reading "Shorncliffe Camp". It was a real scramble as we all piled on to the buses, but Ginger, Pete, Chalky and I all managed to get on the same one. When the buses were full, they moved off one by one. I noticed that some of the young men who'd been on the train hadn't been able to get on the buses and were still standing outside the station. When I mentioned it to the driver, he said, "Don't worry, we'll be back for them."

"At least we'll get first choice on the bunks," said Ginger.

The convoy of buses weaved its way through country lanes. It was the first time I'd ever really been out in the country. There were green areas in London: places like Regent's Park and Parliament Hill Fields and Hampstead Heath, but they weren't really countryside. They were large areas of grass with trees, but you always knew they were surrounded by houses. Out here, the countryside stretched for miles. It was trees and fields, with just a few houses. It was so different from being in London.

The buses reached a gate in a tall wire fence. On the fence was a sign reading "Shorncliffe Camp".

"They ought to take that sign down," said Ginger. "Someone might read it and tell the enemy what's behind the fence. Careless talk costs lives, you know."

We remembered Eric the Miserable, and we all laughed.

The buses pulled up, and we all filed off. A tall man, very straight-backed, with a big handlebar moustache and three stripes on his sleeve – which I knew showed that he was a sergeant, was waiting for us.

"Right, you 'orrible shower!" he yelled in a voice loud enough to be heard back in London. "Line up over there in rows of ten!"

Ginger and I looked at each another, and rolled our eyes. I'd spent years at school with teachers who shouted at me, now I was in the Army with more of them.

"Come on, come on!" the Sergeant shouted. "Don't you know there's a war on? We've got to get you trained double quick so you can get out there and take part in it, so hurry up and get in line!"

We scrambled to get into lines of ten, and once we were assembled, the Sergeant bellowed at us: "Right, atten – shun! Stand up straight, hands by your sides. You're in the Army now! On the command you will march forward, keeping in time, beginning with the first row there!" And he pointed at the line of ten men next to us. "The other lines will follow in single file! Right … march!"

And then he set off, the first ten men following, then our line of ten, then the next, and so on, all the time the sergeant shouting, "Hup two three four … hup two three four."

We marched until we came to the first in a long line of low wooden huts. In front of every hut stood a uniformed soldier.

"Column halt!" roared the Sergeant, and we all stopped.

"First twenty men fall out!" the Sergeant shouted. Turning to the uniformed soldier, he said: "They're all yours, Corporal Rogers."

"Sah!" acknowledged the Corporal, saluting smartly.

"Column, forward march!" shouted the Sergeant, and the rest of the file of men marched off towards the next hut.

"Right, you men!" bellowed the Corporal at us. "You are A Brigade. This is your barracks. It will be your home for the next seven weeks. You will love it and you will keep it clean and spotlessly tidy! Get in, find yourself a bunk, and then assemble outside in two minutes. Go!"

We hurried inside the hut. There were two long rows of ten beds each against opposite walls. Next to each bed was a small bedside table, with a door and a drawer.

"Grab the beds furthest away from the door," said Chalky, hurrying to the far end of the long room.

Me, Ginger and Pete followed him, and the four of us managed to get the group of four bunks at the far end.

"Why do we want these particular beds?" Pete asked Chalky.

"Because when the Sergeant comes in first thing in the morning and starts looking for things to moan about, he'll see the ones nearest the door first. Being this far away buys us a bit of time."

"Yes, but if anything goes wrong, like a bomb hitting us, we're farthest from the door," pointed out Ginger.

Chalky laughed. "If a bomb hits this place, there'll be no need to worry about getting to the door." He tapped the wooden wall. "This place'll just collapse."

The Corporal appeared in the doorway and began shouting: "Come on, you bunch of old women! Stop all that nattering! I told you I wanted you out here in two minutes! Now MOVE!!"

We hurried outside. As we did so, I whispered to Ginger: "This is going to be worse than being at home, being shouted at all the time, and having to do everything on the double. They'll wear us out before we even get to see the Germans, let alone fight them."

Under Corporal Rogers' shouted orders, we half-marched, half-ran to the Quartermaster's stores, where we were issued with a kitbag, uniform, boots, socks and underwear, toothbrush, comb, boot polish and brushes, all the basic things we were going to need. Then we half-marched, half-ran back to the barracks, where we were told to put on our new outfits.

I thought the khaki uniform looked pretty smart, even if the cloth did feel very rough against my skin. The boots were heavy, but I'd been used to wearing boots with metal toecaps as protection against a rusty old car falling on my feet all the time I was working at Uncle George's garage, so they didn't bother me.

After we'd all got our uniforms on, the twenty of us were marched around the camp by Corporal Rogers, who would stop beside a plain wooden building that looked just the same as every other building on the camp, and he'd shout at us, "Ablutions! Latrine block! Showers! Mess block!" or whatever the building was.

"I'll never remember what all these buildings are," groaned Pete in a whisper.

"Just follow the smell," whispered Chalky. "Believe me, you'll find the toilets soon enough, and the mess hall where they serve the food. Those are the two most important ones."

"Stop talking in the ranks!" yelled Corporal Rogers. Chalky shut up, and we carried on with our tour of the camp.

Then, before we knew it, it was time for our first meal. Mashed potatoes and meat. I wasn't sure what sort of meat it was, and neither were any of the blokes at our table.

"Beef," suggested one bloke near Chalky.

"Never in a million years," retorted Chalky.

"Dog?" queried Ginger.

"Urgh!" exclaimed Pete, disgusted.

"How do you know what dog tastes like?" demanded Pete. "Have you ever eaten it?"

"No," said Ginger. "And this meat tastes like nothing I've ever eaten. So it could just as well be dog."

"I reckon it's horse," said another bloke further down. "They eat horse meat in France."

"Whatever it is, it fills a hole," said Chalky, and he tucked happily into his meal.

As I lay in my bunk that night, listening to the other nineteen men in the long wooden hut snoring and making a cacophony of wheezing noises as they slept, I thought of Mum in our tiny house at Selous Mews, and wondered how she was. It was the first time I'd been away from home in eighteen years. I wondered if she was safe.

"G'night, Mum," I whispered quietly to myself. "Stay safe from the bombers."

The next three days all followed the same pattern: breakfast at an early hour, and on the parade ground under the drill Sergeant, who we now knew was Regimental Sergeant Major Mottram, and who claimed to have the loudest voice in the whole British Army. Three days of marching backwards and forwards – quick march, slow march, left turn, right turn, saluting, foot-stamping loud marching, soft-stepping quiet marching – were all accompanied by RSM Mottram's bellowing voice. By the end of the third day we all either had raging headaches, or had gone deaf.

The fourth day brought something different. After breakfast, and led by Corporal Rogers, we were marched to yet another long wooden hut. Inside it looked like a school room: rows of desks and chairs all facing the front, and a bigger desk at the head of the room.

"We're back at school," muttered Ginger.

"Shut up that talking!" yelled Corporal Rogers. "Find a desk and sit down!"

As Ginger and I made our way to a pair of desks next to each other, I thought how much RSM Mottram and

Corporal Rogers, and all the officers we'd come into contact with, reminded me of my Aunt Lou, my dad's sister. Aunt Lou worked in a factory where the noise of the machines was so loud all day long that the women either used sign language to talk to each other, or – if they needed to talk – had to shout to make themselves heard. The trouble was that all of them, Aunt Lou included, carried on shouting when they got outside the factory. When Aunt Lou came to see us she'd sit in our kitchen and yell out even ordinary things like, "Not too much milk in my tea!" so loud that the neighbours four doors away could hear her.

We sat down at our desks, and then the door opened and an officer entered.

"'Tenshun!" shouted Corporal Rogers, and we all got up and stood stiffly to attention.

"At ease," said the officer quietly. "You may sit."

"Sit down!" yelled Corporal Rogers.

We all sat.

"Thank you, Corporal," nodded the officer.

"Sah!" said Corporal Rogers.

With that, Corporal Rogers turned smartly and marched out of the room. All our eyes turned to the officer in front of us.

"My name is Captain James," he told us. "I will be your senior instructor for the next six weeks. You men have been selected for the Royal Engineers because all of you have some sort of engineering skill. We intend to develop those skills to make you a vital part of the Army's efforts to win this war.

"You men are privileged to be joining one of the oldest military units in the country. It began with the military engineers brought to England by William the Conqueror, and has had an unbroken record of service to the Crown ever since. The Engineers have always been at the forefront of all new technological and scientific inventions: telegraphy during the Crimean War, photography during the Abyssinian Campaign of 1867, underwater explosive devices such as the torpedo. It was the Air Battalion Royal Engineers who built the flying machines that led to the formation of the Royal Flying Corps in the Great War. It was also the sappers who designed and built the Royal Albert Hall."

He looked around at us, then asked: "Any questions so far?"

There was the usual sort of silence you get in any classroom when a teacher asks a class that question, and then Ginger put up his hand.

"Please, sir," he asked, "why are the Engineers called sappers?"

Some of the other blokes groaned, just like kids do in class when another kid asks a question, but I was interested in finding out the answer myself.

Captain James nodded. "A good question," he said. "A sap is a trench. In olden days, when a town was under siege, the only way to protect the troops who were attacking it was to dig trenches for them to hide in. The men who dug those trenches, or saps, were the Engineers, and that's how we got the nickname sappers. You will find that very little has changed for the Royal Engineers during the last few hundred years: the piece of equipment you men will be using most will not be a rifle but a spade.

"Much of your training here at Shorncliffe will involve land mines. The different sorts of land mines, how to lay them, and how to defuse them.

"In any battle, sooner or later one side will launch an attack against the other. To prevent our side being caught by a surprise attack, or to slow the enemy attack down, we put mines out between us and the enemy. Two main types of mines are used – anti-tank mines, which explode when a tank track goes over them; and anti-personnel mines, which go off when they're stepped on. Within those two types there are many variations, but these are the ones we'll be dealing with here. We know the way through our minefields, because we have set out our own mines, but the enemy doesn't.

"The enemy, of course, does exactly the same as us to defend their position. So, when our side launches an attack, our tanks and troops have to get through the enemy minefields. In order for that to happen safely, the enemy land mines have to be cleared out of the way and defused. Which is where you chaps come in."

After the lecture, as we walked towards the mess hall for lunch, Pete Morgan shook his head.

"Land mines," he groaned. "I'm going to spend this war finding things that can blow up and kill me."

"Would you rather be in the front line, being shot at by the other side?" demanded Chalky.

"We *will* be in the front line, you idiot," said Pete. "Didn't you hear what the Captain said? That's where these minefields are, right between the enemy and us."

"Oh yeah," said Chalky. "It doesn't sound very safe, does it?"

For the next six weeks we drilled, dug trenches, and learnt about mines.

On our very first day of training we watched from a distance as different sorts of German mines were set off by our training sergeant by fixing a length of string to the trigger of the mine, and then pulling it and setting off the detonator. It was obvious that all of them could do some serious damage.

Over the next two weeks we took apart all different sorts of mines, and then put them back together again, so we would know how they worked and how to deal with them. All of them had dummy detonators and no explosives, so it was completely safe.

Learning about the different types of mine was pretty

bewildering though. The Tellermine was mostly used as an anti-tank mine. Inside it was 10 lb of TNT (a high-powered explosive), which was set off when a tank went over it and pushed down the metal plate, setting off the detonator. The S mine (or "The Schrapnellmine 35", to give it its full title) was about the size of a beer can. Inside the beer can – which was really a small gun – was a small canister filled with 350 steel ball-bearings. The mine was triggered by a three-pronged push mechanism and when this was trodden on, the canister was fired about three feet into the air, where it exploded, blowing the steel ball-bearings 160 feet in all directions.

The Schu-mine was a small anti-personnel mine that only used a small amount of explosive, a 200g demolition charge. The aim of the Schu-mine wasn't to kill, but to blow the feet or legs off anyone who trod on it. It seemed the Germans had worked out that they could cause more problems to our side if they just badly wounded our soldiers, because a wounded man's mates would often try and take care of him while the battle was going on. If he was dead, his body could be left until later.

Then there were the booby-traps the Germans used to stop us from defusing their mines. The typical sort was a wire that went from a pin in the detonator to a peg fixed in the ground. As the mine was lifted, the wire pulled the pin out, and the contraption blew up. The only way to defuse these was to feel for the wire, and then cut it before lifting the mine. It took a long time to clear a field set out with booby-trapped mines.

These mines could be found by using a metal detector, but the Army didn't have many of them. Also, the Germans had come up with a new dodge to make our job even more difficult: a "wooden" land mine. The explosives and the metal shrapnel were enclosed in a wooden casing, to stop metal detectors from finding the mine.

We were also shown how to handle British mines and small bombs.

"Big bombs are dealt with by the Bomb Disposal Unit," our instructor told us. "Their detonators are far more complicated than the ones you're dealing with. They are also much more powerful. The size of mines and bombs we're dealing with may kill or disable a man, or knock out a tank. A big bomb can destroy a whole street. Anyone here who wants to volunteer for the Bomb Disposal Unit and try to defuse something that could blow him into dust is welcome to try."

On the whole, most of us decided to stick with the land mines, though a couple of blokes did volunteer for the UXB (unexploded bomb) brigade. The thing was, most of the work of the Bomb Disposal Unit (BDU) was being done on unexploded bombs that had fallen on Britain. I wanted to get overseas, to where the fighting was going on. All we saw of the enemy in Britain were the German planes when they came over to bomb us. I wanted to fight the Germans face to face.

After three weeks, Captain James made an announcement: "Right, men, you've been playing with toy mines for long enough. It's time to deal with the real thing."

We were taken out to a range and issued with a steel helmet, and a tool kit containing a trowel, a pair of wire cutters and a set of spanners. We also took turns to use a mine detector, which was like a broom handle with a metal plate at the end; a pair of headphones was attached to the plate by a wire attached to the plate. If the plate sensed metal under the surface of the ground, it sent a whining noise through the headphones. The louder and higher the whining noise, the nearer you were to metal. That metal might be a land mine, or it might be just a load of old junk. The only way to find out was to crawl to the place where the metal was hidden, and then scrape away the earth from around it with the trowel and your fingers until you saw what it was.

"Right, men," said the Captain. "In the range ahead of you are land mines, set in rows of four. You will take turns going out in a line of four men, twenty feet apart. When you find your mine, scrape away the earth from around it. If you find a wire, assume this is a booby-trap and it's fixed somewhere in the earth. Cut the wire. Lift the mine out of the earth, and remove the detonator from the explosive charge. Some of the detonators will be held in place by a pin, for others you will need to use a spanner to undo the nut holding the detonator in place. When you've made the mine safe, place it in the two large boxes you will see at the side of the field. Detonators go in one box, the defused mine goes in the other. Remember, these mines are live. Do not knock them, or tread on them, or bang them in any way. Right, first four men … forward."

The four blokes in front, Ted Hoskins, Jack Ward, Terry Nutsford and Joe Latimer, stepped forward to the metal detectors lying on the ground.

"Pick up the detector and put the headphones on."

They did so.

"Right, proceed forward. Move slowly, and listen to the noise in the headphones."

The rest of us watched as Ted, Jack, Terry and Joe moved forward, holding the metal detectors in front of them. They advanced about ten yards, and then Joe stopped. Jack moved forward another pace or two, and then he stopped as well. Ted and Terry hesitated when they saw Jack and Joe stop, but then they edged forward, until they, too, came to a halt.

"You will note, gentlemen, that the mines are not in a straight line," said the Captain.

From our observation point we watched as the four men knelt down and began to scrape at the earth in front of them. I saw Jack reach forward, and then lift up a metal mine. He placed it on the ground, took something out of his tool kit, and set to work on it. A few moments later, he stood up.

Joe, Ted and Terry were still working on their mines. Ted was next to finish, then he, too, stood up, holding the mine in his hands.

"It's a con," whispered Pete next to me. "I bet those mines aren't live at all. It's just done to make us feel what it would be like. They wouldn't be stupid enough to take a chance with real explosives that could kill us."

"Sez you," said Ginger. "Me, I'm not taking any chances."

"That's my point," answered Pete.

I turned back to watching our four mates out in the field. Terry reached forward to pick up the mine he'd uncovered, but suddenly he slipped; he automatically put out a hand to stop himself. The next second there was a flash and a deafening explosion, and then there was just smoke and the sound of Terry screaming.

As the smoke cleared we saw Terry rolling around on the ground yelling in pain, one good hand holding his other arm. His hand had gone – blown off, leaving just a bloody stump.

I felt sick.

"Stretcher, Sergeant!" snapped the Captain.

"Sah!" responded the Sergeant.

Already a medical team was hurrying towards the injured Terry, carrying a stretcher.

"You were saying, Pete?" muttered Chalky.

Pete had gone deathly white, and he looked as sick as I felt. One of the other blokes behind us was already doubling over and vomiting.

"Order in the ranks!" called the Captain.

One of the stretcher bearers gave Terry a shot of something to quieten him down, and another started to fix a tourniquet around his arm to stop the bleeding.

"When you go into combat, doing this job will be even harder," Captain James told us. "You will be under enemy fire. It could well be pitch dark. There will often be noise and confusion all around you. Count yourselves lucky you are learning how to do this job under these conditions here in England, rather than in actual battle."

The stretcher bearers had loaded Terry on to the stretcher and carried him away for proper medical treatment. Ted, Joe and Jack were walking back towards us, carrying their metal detectors. An orderly was returning Terry's metal detector, and the remains of his hand. All their faces were pale.

"Right, next four men," ordered the Captain.

"That's us, Tim," whispered Ginger.

I looked round. Ginger was right. The next four in line were me, Ginger, Pete and Chalky.

We each took one of the metal detectors. I put the headphones on, placed my steel helmet over them, and switched on the detector; I heard a humming noise in my ears. I looked down at the metal detector, and realized that it had spots of blood on it. This was the same detector that Terry had been using. I looked across at Ginger on my left, and Pete on my right, and Chalky beyond him. They looked white-faced. I guessed I looked the same. I still felt sick to my stomach.

"Proceed forward," ordered the Captain. "Move slowly, and listen to the noise in the headphones."

I took a deep breath, and moved forward towards where the mines were. It was lucky the mine detector was quite heavy or my hands might have started shaking. I was scared. Defusing land mines when they were already safe was just playing with toys. These were real, packed with deadly explosives.

Keep calm, I told myself as I moved forward. Keep calm. The humming in my headphones carried on the same low whine as I edged forward, keeping my eyes skinned at the ground ahead of me. What if the detector wasn't working after the accident with Terry? If that was so, then it would keep to the same pitch and I could just step on a mine without knowing it was there.

Suddenly the noise in my headphones altered, going up like a musical instrument changing pitch. There was metal ahead – a mine.

Keeping the plate of the metal detector above the surface of the ground so that I didn't accidentally touch the mine and set it off, I edged forward, listening to the noise in the headphones and scanning the ground in front of me. There it was – a tiny button of metal just poking out of the ground.

I put the detector down and knelt near the button that marked the mine, but not too near it: I didn't want to kneel on it accidentally.

The image of Terry and his bloody stump came into my head again, and once more I felt vomit rising up in my throat, but I forced it down. I was a soldier; I had to control my feelings. I mustn't lose control. The only chance I had of surviving this war was by keeping as calm as I could and obeying orders. I remembered Mum's last words to me: "Come back alive, son." I had to stay calm, which meant putting the image of the injured Terry out of my mind.

I pulled the trowel from my belt. I looked to my left and saw that Ginger was also kneeling by his mine, trowel in hand, looking worried. I looked to my right. Pete was still walking along slowly, holding his mine detector just in front of him. Chalky had found his mine and had started digging around the sides of it with his trowel.

Here I go! I thought. I took a deep breath, and then started scraping away the earth at a distance of about two feet from thesmall metal button, watching all the time for wires in case the mine had been booby-trapped.

I cleared the earth all the way round the mine, and then started to work my way in, scraping the earth away, until finally the mine was revealed. It was an S mine, shaped like a beer can with the detonator sticking straight up from the top like a stick. If the mine went off, 300 metal ball-bearings would explode out of it and tear me in half.

There were no wires attached to it, so it hadn't been booby-trapped. I took a spanner from my belt and set to work to undo the nut holding the detonator in place, all the time aware that if I made one slip I'd set it off. The nut came loose, and very slowly I edged the detonator out, making sure that I didn't trigger the spring that would send the plunger down into the explosives.

Finally it was done: the detonator had been separated from the explosives. There might still be a small spark, but nothing lethal.

I stood up and carried the two parts of the mine, the detonator and the part with the ball-bearings in, over to the large wooden boxes at the side of the field, and carefully placed them inside.

I was sweating like a pig and I had to fight to stop myself from shaking with relief.

Chalky reached the boxes with the two parts of his mine at the same time as me.

"I feel sick," he whispered as he put his mine and detonator into the boxes.

"That makes two of us, mate," I whispered back.

Ginger and Pete joined us, carrying their mines. They also looked pretty shaken, but we managed to force a grin – a mixture of relief and pride at our success – at one another.

We had done it. We had disabled a live mine, and lived. But that had been in controlled conditions. No one was shooting at us. No one was dropping bombs on us. And we had lots of time to disable it. I wondered how I'd cope doing this in a real battle situation, working fast under fire. I guessed it wouldn't be long before I found out.

1 June – 30 July 1942

On 1 June the whole lot of us said goodbye to Shorncliffe and Captain James, Corporal Rogers and RSM Mottram, and set off in a convoy of buses for Folkestone. There, we met our new platoon sergeant, Sergeant Ross, and clambered on board a huge troopship, each of us carrying our kitbags, and set sail for Egypt in North Africa. No one told us what we were actually going to do when we got to Egypt, but I guessed we were going to be defusing land mines.

"You'd think they'd tell us what sort of things we're going to be doing out there," complained Ginger, who felt as annoyed as I did at being left in the dark about what lay in store for us.

"That's the way it is in the Army," said Chalky knowledgably. "They don't tell you anything so that if you're taken prisoner, you can't let on to the enemy."

The cargo holds at the very bottom of the ship, where the tanks and lorries and vehicles and boxes of ammunition were kept, were enormous places, but the areas where we slept were cramped, with low ceilings. Because I was tall I spent most of the first day below decks banging my head against the metal girders, until in the end I learnt to walk everywhere with my head ducked down. Luckily, no one shouted at me "Soldier, stand up straight!" like they did when we were on parade.

Ginger and I sought out one of the ship's crew and questioned him. "How long d'you reckon it's going to take us to get to Egypt?"

"This way round – the long way – about eight weeks," he said.

"What do you mean, 'the long way'?" I asked.

"Right down the west coast of Africa and round the Cape. Then up the east coast of Africa and through the Suez Canal. The shorter way is to go east after the tip of Spain and go across the Mediterranean. That way would only take about two weeks, but of course, we can't go that way."

"Why not?" asked Ginger.

"Because the Med's full of German U-boats and battle cruisers and Italian ships, as well as German and Italian fighter planes bombing every ship that isn't theirs. They're trying to stop supplies getting to our boys in North Africa, which means everything's got to go the long way round. Also, they're trying to put Malta out of action."

"What's Malta?" I asked.

Both the sailor and Ginger looked at me to see if I was joking. When they saw the genuinely puzzled expression on my face, the sailor said: "Don't you know what Malta is?"

"No," I said.

"It's an island in the Mediterranean Sea," said Ginger. "Halfway between the bottom of Italy and North Africa. It's British."

"Right," nodded the sailor. Then, to me, he said, "Didn't they teach you that at school?"

"They didn't teach much at the school I went to, apart from reading and writing and numbers," I said. "We didn't do geography."

"So if you didn't do geography, how come you know where Africa is?" demanded the sailor.

"We did the big places on the map of the world," I said. "Africa, America, the Soviet Union, Europe, China. Places like that. We didn't do small islands."

"Well Malta is very small," said the sailor. "It's also an air base for the RAF. They use the airfields there to bring in vital supplies by plane from England, and then on to North Africa. Plus, we've got fighter planes on the island that attack the ships taking supplies from Italy to Rommel's forces in Africa. If the Germans take over Malta they'll have the whole of the Mediterranean in their pockets, so the Luftwaffe have been bombing it day and night for the past six months, trying to force the island to surrender. The navy have been running convoys across the Med trying to get supplies to Malta for those six months, but most of the ships have been sunk by German fighter planes."

"So what are they doing for supplies on Malta if the convoys aren't getting through to them?" I asked.

"What do you think? They're running out," said the sailor. "No food, no medical supplies, no oil. And all the time the Germans are increasing their attacks. Which is why, with all the German activity there, the Med is definitely a no-no for us on this trip. Otherwise, we could end up being sunk. This route may be longer, but at least you've got a chance of getting to Egypt in one piece."

Ginger and I told Pete and Chalky what the sailor had told us about going to Egypt the long way round.

"Eight weeks!" exclaimed Chalky. "The war in North Africa will be over by the time we get there."

"Yeah, and the Germans will have won," sighed Pete.

"Careful," warned Chalky, "that's treason talk, that is."

"I'm just telling it the way it is," said Pete. "My cousin Mike was in the North African desert and he was brought home in March, just before I got called up. He'd been badly wounded. Lost an arm. He said Rommel's lot are making mincemeat of our boys out there. He said that since last January, our blokes have been pushed right back by the Jerries, right back into Egypt. Mike reckons they can't last much longer, not against Rommel."

"What's all this?" demanded a voice.

We turned to face Sergeant Ross. There was an awkward silence.

"Nothing, Sarge," I mumbled. "Private Morgan was just telling us about his cousin, who was fighting in the desert."

"I heard what Private Morgan said, and I don't want to hear any more talk like that," snapped Ross. "That's the sort of lies and propaganda the Germans want spread about. Well it ain't going to be spread in my unit. Is that clear?"

"Yes, Sarge," I said.

Ross turned to Pete, who looked very shamefaced.

"Is that clear, Private Morgan?" he demanded angrily.

"Yes, Sarge," nodded Pete unhappily. "It won't happen again."

"See that it don't or you'll be on a charge," snapped Ross and he turned and walked off.

We all looked at the very unhappy Pete. "I warned you, Pete," Chalky said.

"I was just saying what Mike told me," said Pete miserably. "And he was there, actually out there fighting in the desert against Rommel and the Jerries. And I bet Mike knows more of what's going on out in the desert than Sergeant Ross, or anyone else on this boat." With that Pete stomped off.

For the rest of that day I couldn't help thinking about what Pete had started to say before Sergeant Ross told him to shut up. That night, just before it was time to turn in, I went looking for him. He was on deck, standing at the rail, looking out over the sea, a thoughtful look on his face.

"You OK, Pete?" I asked.

He turned and saw it was me, and nodded. "Yeah," he said.

"Thinking about your cousin?" I asked.

"What's that supposed to mean?" he scowled.

"Nothing," I said. "I was just curious about what you were saying before Sergeant Ross turned up. About what your cousin told you."

"You heard what Sergeant Ross said," replied Pete. "He told me to shut up about it."

"Yeah, but we'll find out soon enough, anyway," I pointed out. "After all, we're on our way to join the boys out there."

"Then leave it till we get there," said Pete.

"But we've got a right to know what we're going into," I said.

"Then ask Sergeant Ross, or one of the officers," replied Pete. "Maybe they'll tell you what's going on out there. Though I doubt it."

"Why?" I asked. "What's so bad out there?"

Pete hesitated, then he shook his head. "Sorry, Tim," he said. "You heard what Sergeant Ross told me – no talking about it, or I'll be put on a charge. That's good enough for me. My lips are sealed."

With that Pete turned and went back inside. I watched him go, and my head was in a whirl. What was going on in Egypt that was so bad for our side that Sergeant Ross didn't want Pete to talk to us about it?

The next day, at breakfast, I took my tray and sat down on a bench next to Ginger. He was tucking into a bowl of porridge and he had a plate of scrambled eggs waiting. Or, rather, something that looked like scrambled eggs. These days you were never quite sure if what you were eating was what it claimed to be. The "scrambled eggs" were made from powdered eggs that contained some egg, but also had a lot of other things in them to make them bulkier. It was like the sausages we ate – yes, they had some meat in them, but which part of the animal it came from was anyone's guess. Ears and tails and hooves, plus the organs, mixed with oats and water. Still, it was food.

As I ate my porridge, I took a quick look around to make sure we couldn't be overheard by any officers, and then whispered to Ginger: "Ginger, what do you think's going on in Egypt?"

"A war," said Ginger.

"I know there's a war," I said, irritably. "I mean, this business of Sergeant Ross telling Pete to shut up about what his cousin Mike said. You know, about the Germans pushing our blokes back. And then you think about what that sailor was telling us about why we are having to go the long way round to Egypt: because the Germans are sinking all our ships when they try to go across the Mediterranean."

"So?" asked Ginger.

"Well, what are we getting ourselves into?"

Ginger thought about it for a moment, then he shrugged. "Maybe it doesn't do to ask too many questions," he said. "Let's just wait until we get there, eh?"

We finally docked in Alexandria in Egypt on 1 August, eight weeks after we'd set out. All of us were glad to get off that boat.

It was a shock in so many ways. The first shock was finding I couldn't walk properly. After eight weeks at sea, on a boat that had rolled and heaved in the huge waves of the ocean, I'd become used to staggering rather than walking, trying to stay upright every time the boat lurched. It felt strange to find the ground staying firm beneath my feet. For the first couple of days all of us who'd been packed on the boat walked around as if we were just about to fall over at every step.

The biggest shocks, though, were the heat and the blinding glare of the sun. I'd known sunny days in England when Mum and I had gone on holiday to the seaside, but I'd never experienced anything like this. The sun didn't just shine down on you – you almost felt as if you were inside an oven. This was scorching sun, casting sharp shadows against the white walls of the clay-built buildings. At sea it hadn't seemed as bright as it did here on land, where the glare reflected off every surface.

Alexandria was filled with a strange mixture of people: soldiers and airmen and sailors, all walking around in uniform, all talking in different accents – English, Scots, Welsh, Australian, New Zealand, South African, Indian, Greek. Add in the local Arab population, and it was a complete jumble of languages and noise.

Ginger, Pete, Chalky and I went for a walk on our first day. It seemed odd to see modern army vehicles driving through this ancient city which looked like something out of the Bible, thousands of years old: narrow streets packed with white houses, market stalls, bearded men in long robes shouting and pushing, women covered from head to toe, everything being carried on donkeys. There were camels as well, loaded with huge bags of stuff. It was like going back in time. And the smell! I suppose it came from all those camels and donkeys doing their business all over the place, and the fact that there didn't seem to be a lot of water about. I don't think the toilets were linked to a proper drainage system. If they were, then the outlet of the sewer wasn't far away. We went into the *souk*, which was what they called the market, and there was absolutely everything for sale. It made our street markets at home seem pretty poor by comparison. Back in England we had fruit and veg stalls, and stands selling old clothes, and pots and pans all set out in lines. This market was like a madhouse: a maze of stalls with brightly coloured clothes and carpets, fruit of all sorts, and living animals, tied up or in cages. Meat on the hoof, Pete commented.

As we stepped out of the *souk* and turned a corner, an overpowering smell of stale urine hit us. It smelt like the biggest toilet ever, but it wasn't. We had walked into a large square surrounded by the backs of buildings, and in the square were enormous vats made of clay, with men treading something down in them.

"I hope that's not the local wine being trodden from grapes," muttered Ginger.

"No," said Chalky. "It's a tannery. It's how they make leather here in North Africa. They put animal skins in those vats and soak them in urine. They've been doing it the same way for thousands of years."

"How come you know all these things?" I asked.

"I dunno," shrugged Chalky. "People say things, and I just remember them."

The smell from the vats was really getting to us.

"I don't think I'm going to have any stomach for food," complained Pete, holding his nose.

Chalky grinned. "It won't stop me eating," he said cheerfully. "Our house in Newcastle is near the slaughterhouse. This reminds me of home."

We spent four days in Alexandria, and then we were packed into a convoy of canvas-topped lorries and driven out into the desert. Once we'd left Alexandria behind us, the road changed into a track of rock beneath a covering of soft sand, so the lorries kicked up a trail of dust all the way. I was near the back of our lorry so I got a good view of the landscape as we drove along. It was barren. Empty. Now and then a little bush sprouted up from the rocky ground as if determined that it was going to grow, no matter what, but the overall feeling was that this was a dead place: no water, no plants, just miles and miles of sand and rock as far as the eye could see. The road was bumpy and the lorry shook the whole time.

"Does anyone know where we're going?" Ginger asked.

Most of us shook our heads. We'd been ordered to load up all our gear and get on to the lorries, and that was all we knew. I'd learnt that was the way in the Army – no one told you anything. As a soldier you didn't ask why or what or where, you just obeyed orders.

"A bloke in Alexandria told me we're going to a place called El Alamein," said Tully Ward, a sapper from another unit.

"Where's that?" asked Pete.

"It's about sixty miles west of Alexandria," said Tully. "According to this bloke, it's where our boys have retreated to."

There was an uncomfortable silence in the lorry at the mention of "retreating", and I looked at Pete, thinking of what he'd said about his cousin Mike. Pete shook his head.

"I'm saying nothing," he said. "Last time I opened my mouth I nearly ended up on a charge."

We drove on, further and further into the desert, and then I began to notice the flies. There had been flies in Alexandria, but these ones were even bigger. These were huge black creatures that swarmed into the lorries. Soon we were all swatting away at them as they settled on our arms and our faces.

"Ugh!" I exclaimed, as I spat out a fly that had crawled between my lips.

"They're looking for moisture," said Ginger, waving his hands around his head to keep the flies from settling. "Out here in the desert, with our sweat and spit, we're the best chance they have of getting any."

With lots of arm waving, and slapping at the flies with our desert hats, we managed to drive most of them away for a while, but as we went further into the desert, more flies came after us.

Finally, after nearly three hours of bone-shaking travelling, our convoy of lorries pulled up at what looked like an enormous army base. It was larger than anything I'd imagined. It looked like a city of small tents and lorries and tanks that stretched south for as far as I could see.

"This is it, lads," muttered Tully. "El Alamein. The front line."

"How far does it go?" I asked, shading my eyes against the bright sun to look at the line of lorries and tents disappearing into the distance.

"According to this bloke in Alexandria, the front line is thirty miles long, running all the way from the coast down south. This side is us, and about five miles or so in that direction …" Tully pointed westwards "… are the Germans."

"Right, you lot!" bellowed Sergeant Ross, who'd been riding in the cab of one of the other vehicles. "Stop yapping and get down from those lorries! There's a war on and we won't win it by nattering!"

We hauled our equipment off the lorries, and followed Sergeant Ross to the nearest line of small tents – one of the hundreds of rows, like streets packed with houses.

The men we were replacing had already cleared their belongings out of the tents, and were sitting around outside, waiting to board the lorries to set off back to Alexandria. As Ginger, Pete, Chalky and I headed for the tent we'd been allocated, I stopped by the four men sitting outside it, their kitbags and tools stacked up beside them.

"What's it like out here, then?" I asked.

The four men looked at each other as if I'd said something stupid, then one of them grinned at me: "It's great, mate," he said. "It's like being on holiday. All the sand you could ask for. If it wasn't for perishing Rommel bombing the life out of us and making us walk backwards for hundreds of miles at a time, loaded down with as much as we can carry, it'd be a great life."

The other three soldiers chuckled.

"Come on, you men!" bellowed Sergeant Ross. "Less talk, more action!"

As Sergeant Ross moved on to chase up the rest of the unit, the soldier who'd spoken shook his head. "More action!" he echoed sarcastically. "You'll all get action soon enough."

"Right," nodded one of the other men. "Rommel and his army are just five or so miles away, getting ready to attack as we speak. He's pushed us a thousand miles back to here, right across North Africa. He only needs one last push. If he can get through our position here at Alamein, then what's left between him and Alexandria?"

"Desert," said Ginger.

"Exactly," nodded the man. "Nothing but sand. You lot are our last hope."

Just then a sergeant appeared. "Come on!" he bellowed at the four men. "Get on board the lorries. You lucky people are having a rest you don't deserve!"

The soldiers got up, gathered their kitbags and tools, and headed for the waiting lorries. One of them stopped and turned, then gave me a wink.

"Do me a favour, mate. Stop the Germans getting through for as long as you can, will you? After what we've been through, I've promised myself a few days of fun in Alexandria before Rommel gets there."

With that he laughed, and then hurried after his mates.

Over the next few days we got ourselves used to being at the front-line position at Alamein. We were now part of the Eighth Army – the name given to the Allied forces in the desert. It wasn't just a British Army, it was a mixture of regiments and battalions from the different countries of the Empire, mainly Australia, New Zealand, South Africa, India and Rhodesia. The British officers did their best to stop us British soldiers from having too much to do with the other nations, especially the Australians. I found out why one day when three Australian soldiers came into our part of the camp, saying they were trying to set up an international rugby tournament among the soldiers of the Eighth Army.

"The idea is every country puts together a team: you Brits, us Aussies, the Kiwis, the South Africans, and we all put a bit of money into the kitty, and the winners take the loot," announced their leader, a tall, muscular guy who introduced himself as Eddie Kelly. He grinned. "Of course, we Aussies will win, there's no doubt about that. But we need someone to beat to make it interesting. The Kiwis say they'll join in if we can get a few more teams. So, what do you say?"

Chalky shook his head.

"We don't play rugby," he said. "Our game's football."

One of the other Australians sneered. "Football!" he scoffed. "That's a game for pansies. No wonder you Poms need our help in beating this Hitler bloke – you're all soft."

"Some Brits play rugby," said Ginger. "It's just that those

who don't are more intelligent than those that do. We think you have to be pretty stupid to play a game where you get your head trampled on."

"Who you calling stupid?" snapped the Australian, and for a second I thought there was going to be a fight between him and Ginger. Then we heard Sergeant Ross's voice calling out: "You men! What do you think you're doing?"

Immediately Ginger, Chalky, Pete and I snapped smartly to attention. The Australians looked at us, then at one another, shaking their heads.

"Proper little toy soldiers, ain't they?" grinned Eddie Kelly.

Ross had joined us and he glared at the three Australians. "What are you men doing in this part of the camp?" he demanded. "And stand to attention when you're talking to a non-commissioned officer."

The three Australians laughed out loud.

"An officer?" chuckled the man who'd been about to fight Ginger. Then he pushed his face close to Ross's and said, "That's the trouble with you Brits. You'd salute a camel if it had an officer's hat on. Well that's not the way we work. Show me a man I respect and I'll salute him. If he buys me a beer first, that is."

Ross's face grew purple with rage. "How dare you!" he spluttered. "What is your name and regiment, soldier? I'll have you on a charge."

The soldier shook his head.

"No you won't," he said. "No Pommie gives me orders."

Kelly put his hand on his mate's shoulder to calm him down.

"Let it go, Sean," he said. "We're all in this war together, remember. If they don't want to play a game of rugby, forget 'em."

With that the three Australians ambled off, heading towards their own separate camp.

Throughout this exchange Ginger, Pete, Chalky and I had remained standing stiffly to attention. I was shocked at the way the Australian had spoken to Ross. No man in the British Army would have dared to say anything like that, not unless he wanted to face a court martial on a charge of insubordination.

Ross stood glaring after the three Australians, a nerve in the side of his face twitching angrily, and then he became aware of the four of us.

"At ease!" he snapped.

As we relaxed, Ross addressed us, his face grim. "You men are to have nothing to do with those Australians, besides fighting beside them and working with them. I will not have their bad influence spreading through the ranks of my platoon. Is that clear?"

"Yes, Sarge," we said.

When Ross had gone, I turned to the others. "Did you hear the way that Australian spoke to Sergeant Ross?" I said, still shocked. "That was amazing!"

"I heard the Australians have their own way of doing things," said Chalky. "Someone said the ordinary soldiers call their officers by their first names, sometimes even by nicknames. They're like all mates together."

Ginger laughed. "Can you imagine us being mates with Ross and having a beer with him?" he grinned.

"Only if he bought the round of drinks," laughed Pete.

The flies out in the desert took some getting used to. There were no mess tents, which meant that all meals were taken out in the open, and the flies just loved that. I learnt to drink a mug of tea with my hand over the top to keep them out, sipping the tea between my fingers. In an effort to solve the problem of the flies, an order had been issued that every man was to kill 50 flies every day. With them hovering around us by the million, that was easy, you could kill 50 in the space of a few minutes while you were drinking tea. But it didn't stop them, they just kept coming.

The main topic of conversation among the men was the leader of the German Army in the desert, Field Marshal Rommel.

"He's clever," announced one of our mates, Jez Cromer. Jez had been out in the desert for eighteen months, and from him we learnt what had been going on. It was a similar story to the one Pete had told about his cousin Mike, but his time we were hearing it from the horse's mouth.

"When I was first out here there was only the Italians we were fighting," Jez told us. "That was January 1941. There were about 40,000 of us under our Supreme Commander General Wavell, and half a million Italians, but we wiped the floor with 'em. In just two months we took 150,000 Italian prisoners, and almost the whole Italian Army surrendered. Great. As far as we were concerned, that was it, the War was over. And then Hitler sent out Rommel to help the Italians. He brought over a division of tanks – Panzers, they call them – and before we knew what was happening, Rommel started to attack. Not a big all-out attack, but small attacks where he thought we were weakest. And he was right.

"Before we knew it, we were retreating. He was catching us unawares, coming out of the desert where no one expected him. Very cunning. That's why he got the nickname 'Desert Fox'. By July 1941 we'd been pushed right back about a thousand miles, almost to this point here at Alamein."

"And you've been here ever since?" said Ginger.

"No," said Jez, shaking his head. "Wavell was replaced by General Auchinleck, we call him 'the Auk'. He said we were going to fight back. And we did. Last November we went on the offensive and this time it was Rommel's turn to be pushed back a thousand miles, right back to the other side of Libya. Him and his Germans and Italians."

"So what happened?" asked Chalky. "Why are we back here?"

Jez shrugged. "I don't know," he said. "Except that just when we thought Rommel was finished, he launched a counter-attack. January, it was, nearly eight months ago. And try as we might to stop him, he just kept pushing us further and further back, until we landed here." Jez shook his head and sighed. "He's a clever general, that Rommel. He knows what he's doing when it comes to fighting a war. And so far no one seems able to stop him."

The big job that Ross had for me and the lads was filling sandbags and building defensive walls with them. All day long we shovelled sand into sacks and tied them up. When we had a big pile of them we built a wall along the front line of our position. This wall would form a line of defence if the Germans launched an attack and managed to get through the minefields. It was hot, hard and boring work. Still, it was safer than being out in the minefields.

We'd been in the desert for nearly a week, when word came through that a new set of commanders were taking over the Allied Army in North Africa.

"The Auk's been sacked," Tully Ward told me and Chalky.

"Why?" I asked.

"Because he hasn't been able to beat Rommel," said Tully, "and we're back here in Egypt after retreating halfway across Africa, instead of kicking Rommel and his army out."

"Who's taking over from him?" asked Chalky.

"According to my sources, Field Marshal Alexander," said Tully.

"What's he like?" I asked.

"No idea," Tully shrugged. "Never met him. He's going to be the new commander-in-chief of everything. Plus, he's bringing a new commander for the Eighth Army. A general called Montgomery."

"What's he like?" asked Chalky.

Again, Tully shrugged. "No idea," he repeated. "Though I do hear he wasn't first choice for the job. Everyone wanted General Gott. He's been out here before and knows what desert war's like."

"So why didn't they send Gott?" I asked.

"Because he was killed," said Tully. "Didn't you hear?"

I shook my head. "How?" I asked.

"He was on his way here when the Germans shot his plane down. Killed him." Tully shook his head. "So instead we've got a bloke taking charge who's never been out in the desert. What a way to run a war!" As he turned to go he stopped and said, "A word of advice, Tim. Always try and keep up with what's going on. Who's in charge and who's about to get the push. It's all part of staying alive in this war."

"So," said Chalky after Tully had gone. "We've got a new commander. I wonder what he'll be like?"

"Tully doesn't seem to think much of him," I commented.

"Yeah, but Tully's never met him," Chalky pointed out. "He might be good."

"He'll need to be," I said with a sigh. "So far none of them seem to have been able to stop Rommel and his gang."

It was the next day, 13 August, that we got our chance to meet our new commander. We'd just finished breakfast when the signal bugles sounded for Assembly, and we all hurried out to the area of stony earth that was our parade ground. Sergeant Ross was already there when we arrived.

"Right, you lot! Form ranks! Get in line!" he shouted. "Your new commander's coming to see what sort of men he's taken on! Let's try and impress him! Come on, hurry up!"

We all shuffled into our lines beneath the desert sun. Ginger, Pete, Chalky and I were in the line at the front. We'd been standing there for about fifteen minutes, wondering what all the fuss was about, when a jeep pulled up and a thin-faced man with a small moustache got out. He was wearing shorts and a woolly jumper, but what was most noticeable was that instead of wearing a general's cap, on his head was an Australian bush-hat with metal badges stuck in it.

"Are you sure he's a general?" whispered Ginger.

"Quiet in the ranks!" bellowed Sergeant Ross. "'Tenshun!"

We all snapped smartly to attention and Montgomery walked along the lines of soldiers, inspecting us. When he'd finished he returned to his jeep and climbed into the back of it.

"That was a quick inspection," muttered Pete.

But Montgomery didn't sit down. Instead, he turned to look at us, and I realized that he was using his jeep as a platform so he could see us, and all of us could see him.

"Men!" he announced. "I am General Montgomery, the new commanding officer of the Eighth Army in North Africa. So far the fighting here in the desert has been a tug-of-war, with first our side pushing the Germans and the Italians back, and then Rommel and his army pushing you men back to this spot here at El Alamein. Rommel believes that he needs only one more push and he will drive through us and reach Alexandria. If that happens, the war in North Africa will be over and we will have lost. We cannot allow that to happen.

"My orders from the Prime Minister are to destroy Rommel and his army. There will be no further retreating. We will fight on the ground that we now occupy here at Alamein, and if we can't stay here alive then we will stay here dead."

As these words sank in, I could feel a change in every man standing in the lines. No one said anything, no one reacted with words, but we all knew from Montgomery's tone that he meant what he said. No surrender. No more retreat. We stand firm, and we win or we die.

"I intend to drive Rommel and his army completely out of Africa," Montgomery continued. "But we shall do it in our own good time, when we are ready. When we are strong enough to launch an attack, and be able to follow it through.

"But first, we have to be ready for the battle that is about to happen. We know that Rommel is preparing to launch an attack against our position here. It may come in a week, it may come in two weeks. It may come tomorrow. But when it comes, we will stand firm. The Germans must not get past this position. It is up to you men to make sure of that."

With that he nodded to the officers, saluted all of us, and sat down in the back of his jeep. His driver immediately jumped behind the steering wheel, started the vehicle, and they drove off across the shimmering desert.

Sergeant Ross turned to face us. "Right, you men!" he bellowed. "You heard what the new commanding officer said! It's up to you! Orders will be issued later. Dismissed."

As the lines broke up and we walked away, Pete shook his head. "Stay here alive or stay here dead," he grimaced. "It's not our choice, is it?"

"I like him," I said. "He seems to know what he's doing."

"That's the way of generals," said Pete gloomily. "They all have the air of knowing what they're doing. The problems come when they try to put it into practice. I mean, it's all very well him telling us we're going to beat Rommel, but I bet right now Rommel's saying exactly the same thing to his men."

Despite what Pete said, there was no doubt that Montgomery had made an impression on the Army. I found out later that he'd driven round to every division and regiment along the whole Alamein front, giving the same speech about there being no more retreat, and "if we can't stay here alive we'll stay here dead". It seemed to put a bit more backbone into the men and improve morale, as well as scaring the living daylights out of everyone.

The first real impact it had on us sappers was when we were assembled by Sergeant Ross and told we were to enlarge the minefields in front of our positions.

"General Montgomery isn't joking when he says we're not going to retreat any further," he informed us. "So, to make sure that Rommel and his army don't have it easy when they launch their attack, he wants bigger and stronger minefields. Thousands of mines. He wants every German tank that tries to attack us blown to smithereens. Every German foot soldier put out of action before they get to our front lines. So, lads, spades out and let's get digging. And remember, the Germans booby-trap their mines, so let's booby-trap ours. Trip-wires hidden in the ground, every trick you can think of. It's our job to make sure that when the Germans launch their attack, their troops never get as far as us."

And so we set to work. Knowing that the Germans would be watching us through telescopes, and from the air, we started to expand the minefields. Although it wasn't the same as finding and disabling an enemy land mine, it was still dangerous work. Every time you picked a mine out from the vehicle, you were aware that you were holding something that, if dropped or handled wrongly, could blow up and kill you.

We placed the mines like we were sowing plants in a field. The lorry carrying the mines and equipment rolled forward in a straight line, which we kept clear of mines so that we had a track to follow to get through our own minefield. We dug holes, then took the mines from the lorry and sunk them just below ground level across a vast area. We marked it out with lengths of tape so we knew where the mines were.

We set the booby-traps: a length of wire attached to the detonator pin, the other end of the wire fixed to a large pin hammered into the ground. When the German sapper tried to lift the mine clear, the wire would pull the detonator pin and – bang! It was dirty, but they were doing the same to us.

We mixed the different types of mine in the same minefields: anti-tank mines (which were sunk deeper) as well as anti-personnel mines. The German sappers wouldn't find them all. They'd even be able to walk over the anti-tank mines without setting them off.

It took us a week to set out all the mines. Thousands and thousands of them. We needed so many that eventually we began to use German and Italian mines that had been captured. Many of the British ones we were putting down weren't actually made in Britain at all but were what were known as EP mines, or "Egyptian Pattern". The problem was that these were less stable than the ones made in Britain. Metal springs were a vital component of the detonators in

British mines. In Egypt there was a problem making them, so they used a chemical fuse inside a glass phial instead. This meant that EP mines were much more fragile, and had to be handled very carefully.

All the time we were setting out the mines, we kept alert, half-expecting the Germans to attack. But they didn't.

"It'll be night when the Germans attack," said Ginger. "They won't hit us during daylight."

"Rommel's launched attacks during the day before now," Chalky pointed out.

"Yeah, but those were skirmishes," said Ginger. "Like Monty said, Rommel needs just one more big push to get to Alexandria. That means a huge offensive, and he'll want to try to catch us off-guard. Trust me, it'll be at night."

By 25 August all our mines were in place and we sappers joined the rest of the Army in sitting behind our defensive front line, waiting for the Germans to attack. There was work to do for us, of course: making sure our big artillery guns and tanks were all in good working order; checking the supply vehicles over. But mostly we just waited.

It was 30 August and night had begun to fall. Our squad had spent the day laying out even more land mines to defend our front line. Counting the mines the Germans had put out in their own line, there must have been a million land mines between us and the Germans. The gap between the two front lines was a solid mass of minefields over thirty miles long, except for a strip a mile wide between the German minefield at the very front of their position, and ours.

We had finished our work for the day, and Ginger, Pete, Chalky and I were settling down for a quiet game of cards outside our tent, when the alarm sounded and someone shouted, "The Germans are coming!"

Immediately I rushed into our tent and grabbed my binoculars. As I was coming out I bumped into Sergeant Ross.

"Where you going, Jackson?" he demanded. "Bird-watching?"

"No, Sarge, I wanted to see the German advance up close."

Ross stared at me as if I was mad. "How close do you want to get, you idiot?" he snapped. "We're right at the front!"

"Not right at the front, Sarge," I pointed out. "Our tanks and big guns are in front of us."

"Be thankful they are, otherwise the Germans would be using you for target practice," said Ross. "Get your equipment and get with the others. If our guns take a hammering there'll be some nifty repairs needed."

"Yes, Sarge," I said.

With that Ross hurried off. I was still determined to see what was going on, so I put my binoculars to my eyes, and as I did so there was an enormous explosion just to my right, and the force of it knocked me over. A shower of sand and rocks rained down on me.

"Tim, you twit!" I heard Ginger's voice yell.

Then I felt myself being hauled to my feet.

"Here!" said Ginger, and he thrust my steel helmet towards me.

I put it on.

"If one of those rocks, or some shrapnel, had hit you on the head you could have been killed!" he shouted.

He had to yell to make himself heard because the German big guns had opened up now, and heavy shells were either exploding near us, or whistling over our heads and blowing up behind us. Our own big guns and tanks were returning the heavy fire.

"I wanted to see the attack up close," I shouted at Ginger.

"You'll be able to see it close enough if they get through!" yelled Pete.

He pointed out into the minefields we'd laid just that afternoon. Through the drifting smoke, and the light of our searchlights, I could see the German sappers trying to carve a way through the minefields. Their tanks loomed huge and menacing behind them.

"They've reached our minefields already!" shouted Chalky.

Gunfire opened up from our side, tracers poured into the minefields and cut down the German sappers at the front.

"Poor swines," muttered Pete.

"They'd do the same to us if the positions were the other way round," said Chalky.

"The positions will be the other way round soon," said Ginger grimly. "And then we'll be the sappers being shot at."

I put my binoculars back up to my eyes, and found that one of the lenses had been smashed when the rocks had fallen on me. I lowered them and just watched, every now and then ducking down behind the walls of sandbags as German bullets and shells came hurtling towards our position.

The noise was incredible! All thought of talking vanished. Ginger opened his mouth to say something, but I couldn't hear a word. All I could hear was the crashing and booming of explosions as German shells blew up, and the thunder of our own heavy guns returning shellfire and the metallic scream of our machine guns firing.

Behind the barricading walls of sandbags, we were joined by a platoon of infantrymen with rifles ready, bayonets fixed. Sergeant Ross appeared and gestured to us to follow him. The four of us slipped away from the cover of the wall, crouching low as bullets and shells whistled over our heads. As we did so, more infantrymen appeared and joined their mates behind the barricades. They also had their rifles – ready for hand-to-hand fighting if the Germans broke through our defences.

We followed Sergeant Ross to where one of our six-pounder guns had taken a direct hit. Two of the gun crew were lying on the ground and even in the darkness I could see the blood soaking their uniforms. Sergeant Ross pointed at the six-pounder and we set to work, taking off the parts of the big gun that still worked. The idea was that if any other six-pounders took a hit and were wrecked, we might be able to build a replacement from the cannibalized parts. Providing there were the men to man it, of course.

As we worked, a medical team arrived to tend the wounded men. It was obvious from the shake of the head of the medico who examined the two men lying on the ground that both were dead. Meanwhile, the rest of the team set to work to patch up the four other men from the gun-crew as best they could. The seriously injured who couldn't walk were taken off in an ambulance.

As Pete and I worked at unbolting the twisted gun barrel from its mounting, I was suddenly aware of the droning noise of aeroplane engines above us, barely audible above the noise of the gunfire. I looked up and saw a fleet of planes flying from behind our lines towards the Germans. As they reached the German positions, I saw what looked like hundreds of tiny parachutes falling from the planes ... and then suddenly they burst into flames. Parachute flares. Hundreds of burning torches falling down on the Germans, lighting up the night sky as they fell, turning the night into broad daylight.

Another wave of planes followed the first, and they began to bomb the brightly lit targets below. I stood there, awed by the enormity of it, and imagined what it must be like for the advancing Germans: to be caught inside the minefields in the bright lights and beneath the bombs.

But the Germans hadn't given up. There were more whistling sounds above me as their shells came over, and more explosions behind and beside me as they blew up, shaking the ground beneath my feet.

Pete tapped me on the shoulder and jerked his thumb at the twisted gun barrel. I nodded and went back to work with my spanner, loosening the nuts and bolts that held it in place. All the time I was aware that we were under fire with the crash of guns. The air was now thick with black smoke.

I took out the last bolt and Pete and I used brute force to heave the gun barrel away from its mounting. The direct hit on the barrel had pushed it back into the mounting at an awkward angle, but finally we managed to get it free.

Meanwhile, Ginger and Chalky had taken a good gun barrel off the damaged mounting of another six-pounder. Pete and I found them, and the four of us carried this undamaged gun barrel to the good mounting of our battle-hit gun, and bolted it into place. One good gun put together from two damaged ones.

We carried on working in this way, stripping the good parts from damaged guns and stacking them together in neat piles, while the battle continued around us. There was no sign of the enemy troops breaking through our front line.

At 0200 hours, Sergeant Ross came down the line and gestured to us – it was still too noisy for us to hear him speak – to return to our tents and get some sleep. A replacement team of sappers was with him, all kitted up, ready to take over from us.

As I hit my bunk the battle was still going on. The noise should have kept me awake; the fear of being hit by German shells should have kept me awake, or of German troops breaking through our front line and catching me asleep. But the sheer physical exhaustion of the hard work under those conditions meant that within a few minutes of my head hitting my pillow, I was fast asleep.

The next morning, as we all struggled out of our tent to answer the "Reveille" bugle call, the first thing that struck me was the smell of burning metal. It was everywhere, in the hazy smoke that hung in the bright sunshine of the new day in the desert.

As we walked to the parade ground, we passed a unit of Engineers heading back to their tents, finishing their shift and going to bed. Their faces were blackened with smoke and their clothes were stained with oil and sweat. I recognized one of them as Joe Johnson, a sapper from another unit. He looked absolutely worn out.

"Morning, Joe!" I greeted him. "Looks like we won, then."

"No thanks to you lot, all safely tucked up in bed," retorted Joe.

"We were out there before you," Chalky countered. "We were stripping guns under enemy fire while you lot were having supper."

"Anyway, it don't look like we've won yet," said Joe. "One of the tank drivers told me the Germans are massing by that big ridge, getting ready for another go." Joe left us to it, and I looked at the others.

"It's not over," Pete said gloomily. "We've got to go through it all again."

"That's just Joe Johnson winding us up," said Chalky confidently. "The Germans can't have stood up to the hammering we gave them last night. Remember the planes dropping those flares on them? And the bombers? Not to mention our big guns. And just listen…"

We stood there and listened. Nothing – just the

background buzz of an army going about its business, mending its machines.

"See," grinned Chalky. "If the Germans were still going to attack us, we'd have heard about it by now. Trust me, it's over. We've won."

The smile was wiped off Chalky's face as soon as we lined up on the parade ground, and Sergeant Ross addressed us.

"Right, men!" he bellowed. "You did well last night. Those minefields kept the enemy away from our front lines long enough for our big guns and the RAF to do them some damage. But the word is that the Germans are going to try again. It looks like this one will be a daylight attack. So, I want everyone standing by in units as before. Our job will be the same as before: strip and repair all damaged weaponry. If we're going to stop the Germans breaking through our position, we're going to need every gun we've got."

Just as he said those words, we heard a series of dull thuds from the German positions, followed by the whistling sounds of flying shells.

"Incoming!" yelled Sergeant Ross. "Take cover!"

We ran to the low walls of sandbags that offered us protection – just in time as it turned out, a series of explosions erupted as the German shells landed behind our lines.

Immediately our own guns responded, the deafening THUD THUD THUD of their gun-barrels sliding backwards and forwards as they burst into flame and smoke, punching shells towards the Germans.

"Right, men!" hollered Sergeant Ross. "Action stations!"

And so the battle started again, and once more we were up to our sweaty armpits in smoke, fire and explosions and dead and injured men.

It went on like that for five days. Day after day and night after night. The Germans would launch an attack with their big guns and their tanks, while their sappers tried to force their way through our minefields. Our own defences poured red-hot metal at them, keeping their sappers and tanks pinned down, while the RAF flew bomber sorties against them.

As we lined up on the parade ground on the morning of 7 September, surrounded by drifting smoke from the previous night's battle, Sergeant Ross made a different sort of announcement. Instead of telling us, as usual, that the Germans were massing for yet another attack, he bellowed at us: "Good news, lads. The word from our observers is that the Germans are pulling back. We've held them. Well done."

The battle we'd been in for the last seven days became known as the Battle of Alam Halfa, because the main point of the German attack was aimed at the Alam Halfa ridge to one side of El Alamein. Once it had sunk in that the Germans really had withdrawn and it wasn't just a clever ruse on Rommel's part, I felt an amazing feeling of elation – a sense of wonder at the fact I was still alive. We had been in battle, and we'd won. Or, if we hadn't won, at least we hadn't lost. We'd held off the German attack. The minefields that the rest of the boys and I had laid had done their job and slowed down the Germans long enough for our artillery to take good aim at their tanks and advancing infantrymen. The big question now was: what would happen next? We all reckoned that Rommel's forces had taken such a hammering from our defences that it was unlikely he'd launch another attack too soon after the first one had failed. So, when would Montgomery launch his own offensive?

"The end of September," said Pete.

"Why the end of September?" asked Chalky.

"Because of the full moon," replied Pete.

"What, you reckon he's one of those lunatics who's driven mad by the full moon?" asked Chalky, bewildered.

"Maybe he turns into a werewolf," I grinned.

"No, you idiots," said Pete, irritated. "Haven't you noticed that most of the big attacks come when there's a full moon? That's so there's enough light for the attackers to see what they're doing and where they're going."

It had never struck me before, but once I thought about it, I realized that Pete was right. Rommel had launched his attack against us when there was a full moon. So, if Montgomery was using the same tactics, then we'd be launching our attack against the Germans at the next full moon, which, as Pete said, was in the last week of September.

But the end of September came and went, and there was no sign of preparations for an all-out attack.

"Maybe Montgomery doesn't believe in waiting for a full moon," suggested Ginger. "Maybe he's going to go when everything's at its darkest."

"Or attack in broad daylight, when the Germans aren't expecting it," added Chalky.

Pete shook his head. "Mark my words, we'll go when there's a full moon," he said. "Anyone like to place a small bet on it?"

"Yeah," said Chalky. "How much?"

"Two pounds," said Pete.

Chalky shook his head. "Too steep for me," he said. "Five bob?"

"You're on," said Pete, and the two shook on it.

As we moved into the first few days of October, our unit received an order from Sergeant Ross to repair a tank that had been damaged going over a mine.

"What sort of tank is it?" I asked. "I need to know what tools to bring with me."

"No tools that you've got in your box will fit this thing, Jackson," said Ross. "It's a Bitsa."

"A what?" asked Ginger.

"Bitsa this, bitsa that," explained Ross, with a grin. "Its official name is a Scorpion. It's basically a Matilda tank with lots of bits and pieces added."

The Matilda was a two-man tank, a bit smaller than most battle tanks, but with very thick armour.

"What sort of bits and pieces, Sarge?" asked Pete.

"You'll see when you get there," he said.

We loaded our tools into a truck and Chalky took the wheel, heading north under Sergeant Ross's directions. We drove for about five miles, and then we came across a tank sunk into the sand. I could see at once that its offside track had been buckled. What was odd about this tank was that instead of having a large gun mounted on it, it had what looked like a big round drum with lots of long chains hanging down, sticking out the front between two long shafts.

We all got out and gathered round it. The driver of the tank was waiting for us and he grinned as we reached him.

"Hello, mates," he said cheerily. "I've had a bit of an accident with your invention."

"It ain't our invention," said Ginger.

"Well, it was put together by your lot – the sappers," said the tank driver. "Trouble is, when I was giving it a go, I must have missed a mine with the flails."

"What are the flails?" Chalky whispered to me.

"Driver," ordered Sergeant Ross, "start the engine and demonstrate the flails for this lot of ignoramuses here."

"Right, Sergeant," said the tank driver. "Only it won't clear anything because the tank won't move with the busted track."

"We'll fix the track in a moment," said Ross. "Just show them how this thing works."

"Yes, Sarge," nodded the driver, and he clambered up on the tank and disappeared through the hatch inside it.

We all stood and looked at this weird machine for a moment, wondering what it was going to do, when the engine of the tank fired up, and suddenly the drum between the shafts began to turn and the lengths of chain began to spin out, crashing into the ground in front of the tank, beating at the sand and rocks and sending up a cloud of dust.

We all began coughing, and I put my hands over my

mouth and nose to stop myself from choking. Luckily, the tank driver turned off the engine, and then his head popped out from the hatch.

"See it?" he asked.

"And tasted it!" coughed Ginger, and he spat on the ground to get the dust out of his mouth.

"There you have it, lads!" grinned Sergeant Ross. "The Scorpion anti-mine tank! As it moves forward the chains hit the ground and set off any mines lying in front of it."

"So why is it sitting there with one of its tracks buckled, Sarge?" asked Ginger.

"Because the driver can't drive straight," said Ross.

"I *was* driving straight!" protested the driver. "One of the mines must have been deeper in the ground than the others, so the chains didn't touch it."

Pete let out an admiring whistle.

"Well, if they can get this thing to work, it'll put us out of a job," he said.

"That's wishful thinking, Morgan," scoffed Ross. "There is one major problem with this machine which is why it'll never replace you men."

"What's that, Sarge?" asked Chalky.

"If it does hit a mine it stops in its tracks, which means the tanks coming behind it can't get past. On the other hand, if one of you gets blown up by a mine while trying to disable it, the tanks behind you can just roll right over you."

It wasn't a comforting thought.

"Right, you lot," ordered Ross. "I want the track put back on this vehicle, let's get it rolling again. And make a careful note of how you do it, because you're going to be mending an awful lot of these machines before this war's over, or my name's not Ross."

We set to work, first checking to make sure the area around the tank was clear of other mines. As he got out his tools, Ginger looked at the Scorpion anti-mine tank and grinned.

"This is one of the weirdest machines I've seen since I've been in the sappers," he said. "We'd have to go a long way to find anything odder than this."

As it turned out, Ginger didn't have to wait too long to find something stranger than the Bitsa. The day after we'd got it rolling again, Sergeant Ross came into the mess tent as we were finishing our breakfast.

"Jackson, Matthews, Morgan and White," he snapped. "There's a convoy of tanks and lorries heading to the southern position. Grab your kit, get yourself on one of those lorries and once you're there report to Captain Maskelyne, A Force, Royal Engineers. You're joining the Magic Gang."

"The what, Sarge?" asked Ginger.

"The Magic Gang," repeated Ross.

"What's that?" I asked.

"You should know by now, Jackson, that you don't ask questions in this army, you just carry out orders," said Ross crisply.

"How long are we going to be there, Sarge?" asked Pete. "How much kit should we take with us?"

"That depends on how long Captain Maskelyne wants you for," replied Ross. "Just take your usual pack and equipment. Come on, get a move on! This war won't wait for you!"

As we watched Sergeant Ross walk smartly out of the tent, Pete shook his head. "You know, half the time I haven't got the faintest idea what Ross is talking about," he said.

"What's the Magic Gang?" I asked, still puzzled.

"It's a new unit not long been put together," said Chalky. "I heard some bloke in B Unit talking about it. It's a mixture of Royal Engineers and wizards."

"Wizards?" I laughed. "We're going to use magic to defeat the Jerries?"

"That's right," nodded Chalky.

"Here!" said Pete suddenly. "This Captain Maskelyne. Is he the same man who used to be on the stage before the war? The Great Maskelyne, the master illusionist?!"

"That's him," nodded Chalky. "Jasper Maskelyne. He volunteered to help the war effort and they sent him out here to entertain the troops. But then he started to come up with ideas about how he could use his trickery to beat the

Germans, so they made him a captain in the Engineers and set up this new unit, A Force. Known as the Magic Gang."

"What do they do?" I asked.

"According to this bloke, they make tanks and things disappear, and then reappear in the middle of nowhere."

"Pull the other leg, it's got bells on!" jeered Ginger.

"It's true," insisted Chalky.

"Rubbish!" I snorted.

"I saw him performing on stage just before the War," said Pete. "He was brilliant – fantastic! He really did make things disappear. And he sawed a woman in half, right before our eyes. It was incredible!"

"So?" I said. "It's one thing to do conjuring tricks on a stage, it's quite another to make a full-size tank disappear and reappear in the middle of the desert."

"Not just one tank," said Chalky. "He does it with hundreds of tanks. And lorries. He even makes planes disappear."

Just then the tent flap opened and Sergeant Ross looked in and glared at us.

"Are you lot still here?" he demanded crossly. "I gave you an order. Now get your kit packed and get south, or I'll have you all on a charge!"

The convoy was enormous: about 100 lorries and 50 tanks, all heading south in a long line. The four of us sat in the middle of it, in the back of a lorry. Above us, every now and then, we heard the sound of German planes circling us, like vultures hovering over their prey.

"If the Jerries attack us now, we'll be a sitting target," said Pete. "In a long line like this, and in broad daylight, we're like a line of ducks, waiting to be shot at."

"They won't attack," said Chalky. "Reconnaissance only, I bet you. Seeing what we're up to."

"Don't you believe it," said Ginger. "Pete's right. At this speed they could pick us off. They could knock out three or four tanks and the same number of lorries easily."

"Ah, but then the Jerries could lose their planes as well," Chalky pointed out. We all looked at the machine guns set up on the backs of the lorries; the gunners that moved them watching the skies determinedly. "Remember, with all this desert, our gunners have got a clear line of fire at any plane that comes close."

"That's assuming they use fighter planes to attack us," pointed out Ginger. "They could use bombers from a higher altitude. Our machine guns wouldn't be able to touch them."

"At the first sign of their bombers, our RAF boys would be up there, no problem," said Chalky confidently. "I tell you…"

He was cut short as the air around us erupted into gunfire as the machine gunner on the back of the lorry behind ours swung his weapon and let off a burst; streams of bullets poured upwards. I heard the scream of a plane's engine as it came in low and the chatter of bullets from its guns.

"Down!" yelled Pete, and we all threw ourselves on to the wooden floor of the lorry. Not that it would do much good, I thought. The lorry covering was made of canvas and bullets would just tear right through the fabric. However, when you were under attack it was safer to be lying down.

The machine gunners on the lorries swung their guns round and kept up a stream of fire after the German plane as it disappeared into the distance. "All right, alarm over," said Ginger.

The sound of the guns stopped. We all got up off the floor of the lorry and took our places on the crates. As we did so, Chalky went as white as his name.

"Oh my lord!" he said, and for a moment I thought he was going to pass out.

"What's the matter?" I asked. "You've been shot at before."

"Yeah, but not when I've been sitting in a lorry full of explosives," he said. He pointed at the crates we were sitting on. They were marked "AMMUNITION" and "DANGER. EXPLOSIVES".

"Of all the lorries to choose to sit in, we've picked the most dangerous!" groaned Pete.

"Anyway, Chalky," said Ginger, pointedly. "Tell us again how we're not going to be attacked."

Chalky shook his head and wiped his brow. "OK," he said. "A bloke can't be right all the time."

As we journeyed south, we all kept an eye on the sky,

watching out for another barrage from more German fighter planes, but they seemed content with just watching us.

I kept thinking about what Chalky and Pete had said about Captain Maskelyne. I'd never seen him perform, but I'd heard about him, of course. Just before the War the papers had been full of stories about him, with photographs showing him on stage pulling a string of razor blades out of his mouth, or standing around in an evening suit looking handsome. He looked like a film star: he was tall and slim, with black hair slicked back, a centre parting, and a neat pencil-thin moustache. All the women went mad for him. He could do amazing tricks – not just sawing a woman in half and then showing her to be perfectly all right afterwards, or doing incredible card tricks in which he read the mind of the person who'd chosen a card – but once I'd read he even made an elephant disappear from a stage in front of everyone. It was obviously all trickery, but I wondered what sort of magic he was going to use here in the desert, and how that trickery was going to help beat Rommel. The whole idea seemed impossible.

After about fifteen miles we drove past a gang of sappers who were busy digging a trench in the middle of nowhere. Near them were stacks of metal pipes, which were obviously going into the trench.

"Poor blokes," muttered Chalky as we passed them, leaving the sappers behind to carry on digging. I looked out of the back of the lorry and watched the men drop a length of pipe into the trench, then set to work digging up the next section to drop another length of pipe in.

"Why are they laying pipes out here in the middle of nowhere?" asked Ginger.

Pete shrugged. "Looks like they're putting in a water pipeline," he said.

"If they're running a water pipeline to the southern end, it's going to be a long job," I commented. "They're still only halfway there."

Finally, we came to the southern end of the Allied position. The place was buzzing with activity. Men wandered around, there were tanks and lorries, and crates and crates of ammunition and supplies piled one on top of the other. It was obvious that things were building up to a major offensive.

We asked a soldier where we could find Captain Maskelyne, and he pointed to a tall slim figure standing beside a mountain of wooden crates of ammunition. He was holding a piece of paper and talking earnestly with a corporal. As we walked towards him, I realized that we hadn't really needed to ask. Maskelyne looked exactly the same as he did in his photographs, except for the khaki uniform and captain's cap.

Ginger, Pete, Chalky and I walked up to him just as he was stabbing his finger at the piece of paper and telling the corporal: "The point is, Wilson, this thing won't work unless the Jerries *believe*. We have to make them think these things are tanks and not just stacks of crates piled one on top of the other beneath camouflage nets, and for that we need tank tracks coming out from the netting. Tracks that look like this. You can make them with a long broom-handle. OK?"

The corporal nodded. "Will do, sir," he said, and he went off, taking the piece of paper with him.

"Captain Maskelyne?" asked Ginger.

Maskelyne turned to us. "Yes?" he queried.

"Privates Jackson, White, Morgan and Matthews, Royal Engineers, reporting for duty, sir," said Ginger.

We all stood stiffly to attention and saluted.

"Yes, that's quite enough of that," said Maskelyne dismissively. "If everyone spent less time saluting and more time getting on with actual work, this war would be over a lot damn quicker. Engineers, eh? Good. What tools have you brought with you?"

"Just our packs, sir," I said. "Spades for digging, and between us we've got wrenches and hammers and screwdrivers."

"That'll do," said Maskelyne. "Right, you men are going to be privileged to learn the secrets of the magician's trade – something that very few people are privy to. And you are going to help me pull off the biggest illusion of all time."

"Make tanks and planes disappear?" I said.

Maskelyne must have caught the note of disbelief in my

voice, because he jerked his head towards me and fixed me with a steely look.

"And you are…?" he demanded.

"Private Jackson, sir," I answered.

"Well, Private Jackson, the answer to that is yes. For the past few days we have been making tanks and lorries disappear from this point and reappear thirty miles away at the northern point of the Allied position."

We stood in awkward silence. Finally I said, "We've just come from the north, sir, and we haven't seen them."

"Of course you haven't, Private, because they are invisible," said Maskelyne curtly. "And at the same time we have been keeping the non-existent tanks and lorries here in full sight of the Germans so they know they are still here. Even though they are not."

I caught Ginger's concerned expression and I knew he was thinking the same thing as me: we were dealing with a madman. The Great Maskelyne has actually gone mad with all this talk about tanks and lorries being "invisible".

Maskelyne looked at us, his fixed steely look scanning the faces of all four of us as we stood there in stunned and awkward silence, and then suddenly he burst out laughing.

"Oh my, if you could see your faces!" he roared delightedly.

We looked back at him, bewildered.

"Sir?" asked Chalky, baffled.

Maskelyne waved his arm around. "What do you see," he demanded, "all around you?"

We turned and looked at the bustling camp, and then turned back to Maskelyne. "Lots of soldiers," answered Pete. "Thousands of them."

"And?" prompted Maskelyne.

"Hundreds of tanks," said Chalky.

"Thousands of boxes of ammunition," I added.

"Like this one?" asked Maskleyne, and he pointed to the large crate next to him.

"Yes, sir," I nodded.

"Tap it," said Maskelyne.

I looked at him, puzzled. "Pardon, sir?"

"Bang your knuckles against it," he said.

I reached forward and did as he said. The knocking of my knuckles against the wood made a hollow sound.

"It's empty, sir," I said.

"As are most of these," said Maskelyne. "They're brought down by the lorryload, day after day after day, and stacked up, in full view of the German reconnaissance planes."

Then he pointed to a line of tanks hidden beneath camouflage nets.

"What do you see there?" he asked.

"Tanks, sir," said Pete. "Hidden by camouflage nets."

"Go and take a closer look," Maskelyne instructed us.

Puzzled, we went to the camouflage netting, and looked

at the tank. Chalky reached through the netting, and tapped its side.

"Wood," he said in surprise.

"Wood and canvas," said Maskelyne. "Did you drive from the north?"

"Yes, sir," said Ginger.

"Did you pass a party of Engineers digging a trench?"

"Yes, sir," nodded Ginger. "About fifteen miles north of here."

"Why were they digging the trench?" asked Maskelyne.

"To lay a pipeline, sir," I replied. "They looked like water pipes to me."

"And where is this pipeline going to?"

"To here, sir," said Chalky. "At least, that's what it looked like. The trench was being dug from north to south."

"Excellent," nodded Maskelyne with a smile. "In fact you may be interested to know that at night they dig up those same pipes, and the next day, when the German planes are flying over to check on the progress, they carry on digging the trench even further south, laying the same pipes again. There is no pipeline, gentlemen. We are simply creating the illusion of a pipeline. As far as the Germans are concerned, their air reconnaissance tells them that a pipeline is being laid to this position to bring much-needed water here. Their same air reconnaissance also tells them not that we have lots of empty boxes and constructions of wood and canvas hidden under camouflage nets, but that there are masses of crates of ammunition and thousands of tanks here. What sort of message do you think that sends to Herr Rommel?"

"That a major attack is going to be launched from here involving thousands of men," I said.

Maskelyne nodded. "Correct, Private Jackson," he said.

"But … but what about the tanks up north being invisible?" I asked.

"Simple," said Maskelyne. It was obviously giving him great pleasure explaining the mystery behind these great tricks to us. "Next time you go back north, have a close look at some of the piles of crates stored there. You will find that many of them aren't piles of crates at all, but shelters made out of the sides of crates. Inside them are tanks, which can burst out of those shelters in a second. Also, many of the lorries up north are really tanks dressed up with wooden and canvas coverings to make them look like lorries from a distance. And some things that look like mess tents from the air, when seen from the ground actually have tanks inside them."

I had to admit it was brilliant. It was the biggest conjuring trick of all time, and if it worked, it could save hundreds of soldiers' lives. Rommel would think that Montgomery was going to launch his attack in the south, and so he'd put most of his troops there to defend it. When Montgomery actually attacked in the north, there'd be fewer Germans. In theory, it was a great plan.

My three friends and I worked with Captain Maskelyne and his Magic Gang for ten days, building lots of dummy tanks out of wood and canvas. We even made up fake soldiers to make it look like there was some kind of action going on around these "tanks". Every time a German reconnaissance plane came over, we moved the dummies to different positions, so it looked like there were hundreds of soldiers at work, getting ready for the assault.

While we were there, I found time to write a letter home to Mum. Or, at least, a letter for Uncle George to read to her. I'd only written to her a couple of times, once while I was training at Shorncliffe to let her know that I was all right, and once while we were on the boat. I hadn't had a reply from her yet, but I knew that was because she would have to ask Uncle George to write it for her, and Mum wasn't the kind of person who liked to ask for help or to let others see how she felt so I guessed she'd write back in her own good time.

The problem with writing a letter when you're in the Army and there's a war on is that your correspondence is checked by a senior officer to make sure you're not giving away any secrets that might "help the enemy", as they put it. So, we were not allowed to write about where we were, or what we were doing, or if there was any fighting going on, or if any of our mates had been wounded or killed, because any of that information might, apparently, be useful to the enemy.

Also, you were not allowed to write home and complain

about anything, such as the food being lousy, or the flies in the desert making life a misery, because that might have "lowered morale", in the Army's words. Which meant that about the only type of letter you could write home was one that said, "Dear Mum, I'm OK, everything is fine here, we're going to win the War any day now. Love from your son, Tim." Still, at least a letter from me would let her know that I was still alive and well enough to write. So, I wrote and told her I was out in the desert (though I expected the officer who'd be checking it would cross that out), and that I was well, and I was thinking of her, and hoping she was keeping safe, and I was looking forward to seeing her at home soon.

About the middle of October the lads and I got orders to return to the north, back to El Alamein itself. This time round, our journey with the convoy was safer, travelling at night, with no lights, moving slowly enough to see the vehicle in front so there was no risk of a collision. A hundred lorries and a hundred tanks, moving back to the northern position under cover of darkness, at a time when the German reconnaissance planes wouldn't be up and flying and able to see what we were up to.

"So, what do you reckon to the Great Maskelyne, Tim?" asked Ginger as we travelled north.

I shook my head in admiration. "He's a genius," I said. "To hide a whole army in one place, and have a pretend army in another, and in the middle of a desert where the Germans can see what's going on. It's absolutely fantastic!"

"Beats making an elephant disappear on stage at the Palladium," nodded Pete.

"It's only fantastic if the Germans fall for it," said Chalky.

"We fell for it, and we were right up close," I pointed out. Pete and Ginger nodded in agreement.

"Yeah, but we're not Rommel," said Chalky. "He's a clever one, that Desert Fox. I bet he's got a few tricks up his sleeve as well. Maybe he's got his own magician working for him. What do you think about that?"

I fell silent and thought about what Chalky had just said. It was a good point. Rommel was clever, there was no doubt about that. They didn't call him the "Desert Fox" for nothing. So far he'd outwitted every British general who'd come out to the desert to try and beat him. Montgomery was being very clever using Maskelyne the Magician to decoy the Germans into thinking the major attack was going to come from the south. But what if Rommel didn't fall for it? What if he had his own sneaky plans, which at that very moment he was putting into operation without us knowing about it?

As soon as we got back to the main Alamein position, we realized that the easy-going days with Captain Maskelyne and the Magic Gang were over.

"Right, you lot," bellowed Sergeant Ross in greeting. "Your life of leisure is over! You're back among the workers now, so, get yourself equipped with a long-handled shovel from the stores and report back to me."

"A long-handled shovel," groaned Pete. "This is going to mean some serious digging."

"Not at this hour, surely!" exclaimed Chalky. He checked his watch. "It's nearly nine o'clock at night. I bet he's just going to give us our orders for first thing in the morning."

As so often, Chalky was wrong.

We reported back to Sergeant Ross and he pointed to an area marked out with tape. "We're digging trenches," he told us.

"At night, Sarge?" asked Chalky.

"Of course at night!" shouted Sergeant Ross. "We don't want the Germans watching us and knowing what we're up to, do we?"

"I bet this is another of the Great Maskelyne's tricks," Ginger whispered to me out of the corner of his mouth.

"You are going to dig trenches deep enough and long enough for a platoon to hide inside," continued Ross. "As you will be the men hiding in it, I'd advise you to make sure the walls are strong and won't collapse on you when you're inside. These trenches have got to be deep enough for a man to stand up inside them without his head poking over the top, because we're going to put canvas roofs on them so the Germans won't spot them when they fly over. Any questions?"

"Yes, Sarge," said Ginger. "What are these trenches for?"

"When I say 'any questions', Private Matthews, I am simply being civil. I do not expect you to ask one! Now, get to work."

We started digging a series of trenches eight feet deep. It was hard work. The ground was rocky and tough in some places; in others it was just loose sand. Although the sand was easier to dig, it was impossible to make a wall from it that wouldn't collapse, so we had to shore it up with timbers. The rocky ground was even worse, because when you dug the rocks out, it was just sand again, which also collapsed.

We spent the next week resting during the day and digging every night. As we dug, we talked about what the trenches might be for.

"Montgomery's hiding the Army up here," said Ginger.

"Like I said, I bet this is one of Maskelyne's tricks. The soldiers up here hide in the trenches under the canvas roofs and they're invisible from the air. So, Rommel thinks the bulk of the Army is down south, where all those dummies are."

"But Ross said that *we're* the ones who are going to be hiding in these trenches," pointed out Chalky.

"Of course he'd say that," countered Ginger. "He wants to make sure that we make these trenches safe enough for us to stay in."

We finally found out what the trenches were for on the morning of 23 October. The whole of our division of Royal Engineers were assembled on the parade ground, and Captain Medley, our commanding officer, came to address us.

"Men," he began, "I have been authorized by our commander-in-chief, General Montgomery, to tell you that tonight we will be launching a major offensive against the Germans. We have kept this information secret until this moment to prevent the Germans finding out.

"Late this afternoon you will go into the trenches you have dug at the front of our position. The RAF will fly covering actions to prevent any German reconnaissance of this movement. You will take with you all your equipment, and a packed dinner. You will be there for some hours, concealed beneath the canvas roofs.

"At 2140 hours, our artillery will open fire on the positions of the enemy's big guns, which are to their rear. It will be one of the biggest bombardments there has ever been and we intend to put the German big guns out of action. This bombardment will last for twenty minutes.

"At 2200 hours our artillery will switch the bombardment to the very front of the German positions. You men will then come out of the trenches and advance through our own minefields, clearing a path for our infantry and tanks, which will be close behind you. You will continue advancing until you reach the defensive minefields laid by the enemy. You will clear a path through the enemy minefields in order that our infantry and tanks following you can get clear sight and attack the enemy."

I felt a knot in the pit of my stomach as what Captain Medley said sunk in. In less than twelve hours, we were going right into the enemy firing line. I couldn't help but give a little shudder at the thought. I hoped no one noticed.

Captain Medley continued his address to us, but now his voice took on a much more serious tone.

"I know I'm speaking to young men, some of you only eighteen or nineteen years old, but I have to give it to you straight," he said. "Some of you will be killed, or lose an arm or leg, because Jerry will be trying to stop you. There will be mortaring, Stuka dive bombing and plenty more besides. But you have to open a path through the minefields for our tanks and our infantry, or else this battle will be lost. And if we lose this battle, gentlemen, there is a strong possibility we shall lose this war. And that must not be allowed to happen. We cannot let the evil code of the Nazis rule this world and destroy everything that we hold dear.

"I will now hand over to Sergeant Ross, who will detail the tactics that will be used to open pathways through the minefields tonight. Sergeant Ross."

"Thank you, sir!" thundered Sergeant Ross. "Right, lads, this is the plan for tonight's attack. In order to get the tanks rolling, we need to clear a series of paths twenty-four feet wide through the minefields, and we need to do it fast. The boffins at the top reckon a team of six men can clear a gap eight feet wide using a metal detector. By their way of thinking, that team of six should be able to move forward at the rate of nine feet a minute. Which is three times faster than clearing mines by poking a bayonet in the ground and trying to find them. The six are: one man using the metal detector, one who'll lift and disable the mine, two men who'll be marking the side of the cleared path with tape so the tanks can see where they're going, and two men in reserve. So, three teams of six men each should be able to clear a gap twenty-four feet wide at the same speed, nine feet a minute. Any questions?"

Ginger put up his hand.

"Yes?" demanded Sergeant Ross.

"If it's going to be dark, how will we see to clear the mines at that speed, sir?" he asked.

"Because, you lucky lads, you will have searchlights on you the whole time. It will be like daylight out there."

Pete put his hand up.

"When I asked for questions I didn't expect everyone to put their hands up," complained Ross. "This will be the last question. Yes, Morgan?"

"If we're going to be lit up by searchlights so we can see, then won't the enemy be able to see us as well, Sarge?" asked Pete. "I mean, if they can, they'll have a clear target for shooting at us."

"If I may answer this question, Sergeant," said Captain Medley.

"Certainly, sir," said Ross.

"As I said earlier, before you go out and start clearing the minefields, our heavy artillery will launch a bombardment of the enemy positions to protect you," said the Captain. "It is unlikely the enemy will have any chance of shooting at you while that bombardment is going on."

"Thank you, sir," said Ross. "I think you have put any concerns the men may have had to rest." Looking at Pete, he snapped, "And even if the Germans do shoot at you, Morgan, you can't have everything. This is war, remember." Turning back to Captain Medley, Ross asked: "Are there any further points you wish to make to the men, sir?"

Medley nodded. "There is just one last point, Sergeant," he said, and he produced a sheet of paper. "The Commander-in-

Chief, General Montgomery, has written a personal message to all the men in this Army. It gives me great pleasure to be able to read it to you all."

At this, Sergeant Ross stamped to attention. "Right, squad!" he yelled. "You are about to hear a personal address from General Montgomery. You will all pay careful attention."

"Thank you, Sergeant," said Medley. "These are the words of General Montgomery himself, addressed to every one of us," Captain Medley informed us. Then he began to read from the sheet of paper:

"When I assumed command of the Eighth Army I said that the mandate was to destroy Rommel and his army, and that it would be done as soon as we were ready. We are ready now.

"The battle which is now about to begin will be one of the decisive battles of history. It will be the turning point of the War. The eyes of the whole world will be on us, watching anxiously which way the battle will swing. We can give them their answer at once, 'It will swing our way.'

"We have first-class equipment: good tanks; good anti-tank guns; plenty of artillery and plenty of ammunition; and we are backed by the finest air striking force in the world.

"All that is necessary is that each one of us, every officer and man, should enter this battle with the determination to see it through – to fight and to kill – and finally, to win. If we do all this there can be only one result – together we will hit the enemy for six, right out of North Africa.

"The sooner we win this battle, which will be the turning point of this war, the sooner we shall all get back home to our families. Therefore, let every officer and man enter the battle with a stout heart, and with the determination to do his duty so long as he has breath in his body.

"And let no man surrender so long as he is unwounded, and can fight.

"Let us all pray that the Lord mighty in battle will give us the victory."

Captain Medley folded up the sheet of paper and put it in the pocket of his tunic. "That is the message from our commander," he said.

"Bear those words in mind when you go into battle tonight." Turning to Sergeant Ross, he said: "That is all, Sergeant."

"Thank you, sir!" bellowed Ross. To us, he yelled "'Tenshun!"

We all sprang to our feet and stood stiffly to attention.

"Squad, dismissed!" roared Ross.

1700 HOURS 23 OCTOBER – 24 OCTOBER 1942

That afternoon, RAF fighters zoomed around in the sky above us to keep away German planes, and lorries drove backwards and forwards throwing up dust clouds to stop the Germans seeing what was going on through their telescopes. At 1700 hours we climbed down into the long slit trenches right at the very front of our position, and sat down on the seat-shaped sections of rock and sand. We were in groups of six, just like Sergeant Ross had told us we would be. Our team of six included Ginger using the metal detector, me as the one who'd be down on his hands and knees disabling the mines, Pete and Chalky laying the tape to mark the way for the tanks, with Billy Paul and Joe Johnson as reserves in case something bad happened to any of the four of us. Billy and Joe also had rifles ready with bayonets fixed to act as probes if the metal detector packed up, or got blown up.

By 1740 hours we were all in place; the trenches were filled. The lorries stopped their mad skidding around on the desert and outside the trenches the dust clouds died down.

Above us the sheet of canvas that hid the trenches from the German telescopes flapped slightly in the afternoon breeze.

"Four hours to go before the bombardment starts," said Ginger, checking his watch. "What shall we do?"

"We could play I-spy," suggested Pete.

"That shouldn't take long," said Ginger with a laugh. "I spy with my little eye something beginning with S."

"Sand," said Pete.

"Exactly," grinned Ginger.

"I don't know about you lot, but I'm going to eat my packed dinner," said Chalky. And he started to unwrap the greaseproof paper from his sandwiches.

"How can you eat at a time like this?" demanded Pete.

"Because I don't know if I'll feel like eating later," said Chalky.

That made sense. Ginger nodded and began to unwrap his own sandwiches.

I left mine untouched. I felt too sick to even think of food. In my head I kept seeing the images of those German sappers when Rommel had tried to launch his big attack at Alam Halfa. Saw them falling as our machine guns cut into them, or being blown up as they lifted a booby-trapped mine. Was it going to be the same for us? Captain Medley said the bombardment from our big guns would keep the Germans down. But then, he would say that, wouldn't he?

I wished I had more than just a steel helmet to protect me

from the bullets. I was wearing shorts and a cardigan. They were the right clothes to wear against the cold of the desert night, but not against bullets. And not against exploding mines.

But Captain Medley had been honest with us. Some of us were going to die. Some of us were going to be seriously wounded. Would one of them be me? I wished I'd written more in my letters to Mum. More about how grateful I was to her for bringing me up on her own, and how much I missed her. If I was going to die, I wanted to see her one last time and tell her I loved her. But now it was too late.

As I watched Ginger and Chalky munch their sandwiches, I felt around in my pack for a stub of pencil and a piece of paper. Then I wrote, "Always thinking of you, Mum. Thanks for everything. You are the best Mum in the world. Your loving son, Tim." I folded the piece of paper over and wrote her name and our address on it. Then I nudged Ginger, who was sitting next to me.

"What's up?" he asked.

"Will you do me a favour?" I asked.

"Sure," he said. "What?"

"If I don't make it out of this, and you do, will you give this note to my mum?"

I offered him the piece of paper. Ginger nodded, took it, and tucked it away into his breast pocket. "Sure," he said. "But you'll come out of it all right. The Germans haven't got you yet, have they?"

But even though he said the right words, I could tell from something in his voice that he didn't really mean it. None of us knew what was going to happen to us tonight. None of us knew if we were still going to be alive tomorrow. We sat there in the trench as darkness fell.

The hours passed. As the hands of my watch ticked nearer to zero-hour, I could hear some of the blokes in the trench muttering to themselves, and I realized that they were saying prayers. Some were praying for themselves, others were praying for their families back home. Most of them, though, were like me, just sitting in silence and waiting.

And then, right on the dot, the barrage from our big guns started, and it was like nothing I'd ever heard before. It was huge. No, huge was too small a word for what was happening, for the sound and the vibration of the earth around us. It was as if the whole world had suddenly gone into one enormous explosion as we pounded the enemy, sending shell after shell overhead, the earth lifting and falling with the incessant thudding. For a moment I was worried that the trench was going to fall in on top of us.

With all that noise there was no way we could have talked even if we'd wanted to. For twenty minutes the barrage went on and then there was a sudden switch in the noise as our guns turned their attention to the German front line. I looked at my watch – 2200 hours.

I felt a tap on my knee and looked up. Ginger was

standing up and gesturing to me that it was time to go. I tapped the man next to me for him to pass the signal on, and then I followed Ginger and the long line of men. Up the steps we went, out of the trench, and into a night that could have been daylight. Above us was a bright full moon, and I remembered what Pete had said. He was right about generals attacking by full moon. He had won his bet with Chalky. Searchlights from our own side blasted dazzling light into our defensive minefields, and on towards the German lines.

Here we go, I thought.

We were five miles from the German front line, so I calculated we should be out of danger from their machine guns until we reached their minefields.

Clearing our own minefield wasn't too bad. We knew where the mines were – we'd already marked them all in preparation for this – but we still used the system that Sergeant Ross had explained: six men working as a team to clear a gap eight feet wide using a metal detector. To our left another team of six were working to clear their own eight-feet wide gap, and to our right another team of six was doing the same. Eighteen men making a gap of twenty-four feet. Wide enough for a tank to get through.

Because we knew where the mines were, Billy Paul and Joe Johnson joined me in defusing them and putting them in a trench to one side of the minefield. Ginger still worked with the metal detector, and Pete and Chalky laid the lengths of tape to mark the edge of our cleared section.

I was lifting one of our mines when there was an explosion from the team to our right. I only heard it because there had been a momentary lull in the barrage from the big guns. We all looked, and saw that the man lifting the mines had handled one incorrectly, and it had exploded. Luckily for him, the charge in the mine wasn't big enough to kill him, but I could see that his leg had been blown off. He was thrashing around on the ground and screaming in agony. Then the big guns of our artillery opened up again. I turned back to my own mine-clearing and tried to forget the image of the wounded man. I had to keep my hands steady and my nerves calm. I had to get this right.

Our team worked its way forward, the earth around the mines being scraped away, the detonators taken out, then the mines lifted clear and put to one side in the trench behind the marking tape.

The ground around me was shaking now, and I looked behind me to see our infantry, their bayonets fixed, following us. Behind them came our tanks, which was why the ground was shaking.

Yard after yard we cleared, and then suddenly we were out of our own minefields and heading across the patch of no-man's land towards the barbed wire that marked the beginning of the German minefields. Ginger went ahead first with the metal detector. Although there should have been no mines in this patch of ground, we couldn't afford to take anything for granted.

Behind us there was the constant sound of firing as our artillery and tanks kept up their bombardment of the German front-line positions, shelling them to stop them firing at us, but the Germans fought back. Tracers of bullets came from their lines, smacking into the ground in front and around us. The terrifying thought struck me that if one of those bullets hit a mine near me, I'd be dead, but I did my best to push the thought away. It was as Captain Medley had said, we had to force a way through their minefield for our troops to be able to attack the Germans. If we didn't, they'd win this battle – and maybe even the War. We had to go on.

We reached the German barbed wire and I knelt down on the ground, took out my wire cutters and cut through the strands of wire to open up my section. The guys on either side of me were doing the same. All the time there was the sound of machine-gun fire and bullets picking at the ground or going over our heads. Frantically I tried to remember our lessons on the maximum range of German machine guns. It was supposed to be no more than a mile, but bullets were hitting the ground around me. The German barbed wire was supposed to be two miles from their most forward position, so either they had machine guns that could fire further than we thought, or Rommel had moved some of his defensive machine-gun posts a long way forward, right into the middle of their minefields.

Behind me the infantrymen began to open fire over our heads and through the spaces between us, aiming at the unseen German lines ahead. Our tanks also began to launch their shells and they hurtled over us into the darkness. The noise was excruciating.

As we worked, the gunfire got more intense. I felt a glancing blow on my head, and heard a metallic "ping!" as a bullet from a German machine gun ricocheted off my steel helmet. I was glad I was wearing it or that bullet would have taken off the top of my head.

We kept low now: Ginger on his knees, holding the metal detector in front of him, while I crawled along the ground, trying to keep below the stream of bullets from the Germans. Now and then one of our tanks got a hit on a machine-gun post, and the firing from the German lines stopped. But it was a momentary relief: soon a replacement crew would pick us out and the firing would start again. Bullets tore at the rocky ground, sending slivers of rock and sand up into my eyes.

I heard a thud and a gasp from my left and turned in time to see Ginger crumple and collapse. In the light from the searchlights and the moon, I could see a dark stain spreading across his shirt. I hurried over to him to see where he'd been hit, but one of the infantrymen grabbed me and pointed ahead towards the German lines. Billy Paul was already hurrying forward to pick up the metal detector that had fallen from Ginger's grasp as he was hit. I hesitated, not wanting to leave my pal, then realized that the infantryman was right: the troops and tanks had to get through.

Billy had taken the headphones off Ginger's head and put them on, and now he moved forward, holding the metal detector in front of him. He stopped and pointed at a small bulge in the ground. I nodded. A mine was there, hidden just below the ground. I set to work with the trowel, scraping the earth away as quickly as I could, but carefully in case it was booby-trapped. It was. A wire went from the detonator to a spike in the ground. I cut it with my wire-cutters and then went on to disable the detonator. I wanted to go back and see how Ginger was. Had he been killed? If he hadn't – if I helped him – could I save him? But if I did that I'd slow down the whole process, and we had to get the paths through the minefields cleared before the Germans had time to react fully. I clenched my teeth and moved on with Billy, both of us on our knees. All the time our soldiers kept up a stream of gunfire over our heads into the German positions, with the tanks behind us loosing off a shell every now and then, blasting away at the Germans.

I had no idea how long we'd been working; it all seemed

to merge into a blur of noise and death, and I was caught in the middle. There was no way back, all I could do was go on.

We kept moving, going as fast as we could. All around us were explosions. I didn't know if they were mines going off as they were lifted by our men, or mines accidentally stepped on, or explosions from German artillery being fired at us.

We reached a German machine-gun post. The crew were all dead, lying around the blasted remains of their gun. The gunfire from the German lines was getting heavier. We were getting closer every step. And then suddenly there were no more mines. There was the wreckage of guns and machinery, burning tanks and lorries and vehicles, and dead bodies lying on the ground, but no more mines. We had cut our path through the German minefield.

The artillery men behind us began to pour forward at speed, firing as they went, sending a hail of bullets into the German positions.

Pete, Chalky, Billy, Joe and I moved to one side as our tanks surged past us and began to roll through behind our infantrymen, into the German stronghold.

We had broken through.

24 October 1942 – April 1943

While the main attack by the infantry and the tank regiments continued, we sappers pulled back to our base. The Germans were still firing, loosing off artillery shells and stray machine-gun bullets, which meant we had to keep our heads down, but at least we could move faster, sure that the ground in front of us was clear of mines. Not that there was a lot of room for us to move, with the infantry surging forward and tanks rumbling past us and nearly running us down.

As I moved back towards our own lines, ducking my head and crouching low the whole time, I scanned the ground, looking for Ginger, but there was no sign of him. I saw a couple of stretcher-bearers carrying away a wounded man and thought it might be Ginger, but when I got near them I saw it wasn't. I tapped the nearest stretcher-bearer on the shoulder. With all the gunfire and explosions going on it was hard to make myself heard, but I put my mouth close to his ear and shouted: "Have you seen a wounded bloke with ginger hair? One of our mob? A sapper?"

The stretcher-bearer shook his head sadly.

"Wounded blokes are all I've seen, mate," he said.

"He was shot somewhere round about here," I said, gesturing at the area around us.

The stretcher-bearer shook his head. "Sorry, mate," he said. "Someone else might have picked him up."

I made my way back through the lines of advancing infantry and rumbling tanks, looking all the while in case I could see Ginger. But by the time I got back to our own positions, I'd seen no sign of him.

The first person I ran into when I got back was Chalky.

"Where have you been, Tim?" he asked. "We thought you'd been caught out there."

"I've been looking for Ginger," I said. "I wondered if the first-aid people had found him."

Chalky's face fell. He nodded.

"Yeah," he said, dully. "They found him. They brought him in."

"Where is he?" I asked urgently.

"In the morgue tent with the others," he said. "He's dead, Tim."

I felt as if I'd been hit by a hammer. Ginger, dead. I felt so guilty. I wondered if I'd stopped and helped him instead of going on, clearing mines, he'd still be alive.

Chalky must have seen what I was thinking from the expression on my face, because he said: "He died straight away. Bullet through the heart. There was nothing any of us could have done to save him, Tim."

I nodded, but it didn't make me feel any better.

The attack continued for the rest of the day. While our infantry and tanks pushed forward, we sappers went into the minefields and collected up the mines and detonators we'd discarded the night before, and loaded them on to lorries. There were hundreds of thousands of them. All different types – British, German, Italian, and some I'd never seen before.

As I lifted the mines and packed them into the lorries, I thought of Ginger, and how there was no sense in any of it. Who lived and who died. It was all chance. Ginger and I had been side by side, but it had been Ginger who died and me who lived. Why? You did your best to keep yourself safe, but in the end it was all down to luck.

I kept thinking of that first day I'd met Ginger, at London Bridge station. I'd liked him straight away. He was friendly and honest and open and cheerful. And clever. Much cleverer than me. And now he was dead at eighteen years old. It didn't seem right.

Although we'd broken through their minefields, the Germans held firm. For the next week we threw everything we had at them: tanks, heavy artillery, the RAF bombing them day and night, the infantry, but still we couldn't get past them, and they wouldn't retreat – they just stayed there and took a blasting. And then, on 4 November, the news came that the Germans were retreating. But it took a lot longer before it was over. They only retreated about 50 miles, and then they started to set up their defences. Although there were fewer of them than there had been at Alamein, they did everything the same as before: laid out minefields in front of their front-line position, dug in their heavy artillery, and kept their tanks ready to defend against attack.

We all thought that Montgomery would go straight after Rommel and not give the Germans time to dig in like this, but he didn't.

"I don't understand it," I said to Pete and Chalky one day in the mess tent, as we listened to reports from the RAF reconnaissance planes that said how the Germans were building up their defences. "Why don't we go after the Germans now, straight away?"

Jez Cromer, who was just along the table from us, answered: "That's because Monty's learnt from where things went wrong before."

"How?" I asked.

"Remember I told you we pushed Rommel right back, and then he pushed us right back?" he asked.

I nodded.

"Yeah," I said.

"Well that's because every time we thought we'd got him down and out for the count once and for all, he came back at us and knocked us out. What Rommel'd do is sit tight, then he'd send out a skirmishing squad of his tanks to attack us.

Then they'd turn and run, and we'd go after them, set on getting them before they got away. That's what Rommel was waiting for. As soon as our tanks and attack force was out in the open – wham! He'd hit us and knock us out, and then he'd counter-attack and send his tanks into the hole he'd made in our defences.

"Mark my words, Monty's not going to play into his hands like that. Remember what he told us before Alam Halfa? That he was going to wait and attack the Germans when he was ready, not before. The Germans may have lost a lot of men and equipment at Alamein, but so did we."

Yes, I thought. Ginger among them.

"We've got more men and tanks and ammo due in from Alexandria," Jez continued. "My bet is Monty's going to wait until we're back up to strength before attacking Rommel."

Jez was right. And not just about attacking the Germans at their new position. We hit them hard there, and they pulled back again. And once again, Monty waited until we were up to full strength before he launched his attack.

It took another six months of battles fought in this way before we finally forced the Germans to surrender. Six months of us attacking, the Germans retreating and digging in, then us waiting until we were strong enough to launch another attack. Each time it was the same form: our side opening with an enormous barrage from our heavy guns and tanks on the German positions; then we sappers would go in and clear the minefields the Germans had laid out; then our infantry and tanks would attack and force the Germans back another fifty miles or so, where they would dig in again. Each time there were fewer of them. Each time Monty would wait until he'd got more reinforcements of men, more supplies of ammunition, before attacking again.

How those Germans held out, I don't know. By the end they must have been down to just a few thousand men, but they were fighting every step of the way as they retreated. The end came on 12 May 1943 at a place called Tunis on the North African coast, 2,000 miles west of Alamein. The Germans must have been hoping that the enemy navies would take them off the harbour at Tunis and get them home, but the RAF kept up such a force of bombing on the German and Italian ships that in the end what was left of Rommel's army had no place left to go, so they surrendered.

The rest of the boys and I carried on under Monty's command, across the Mediterranean Sea to Sicily. By now we had teamed up with the Americans, who'd been fighting their way across Africa from the west, and our joint force launched an attack on Sicily where the Germans and Italians still had a strong base. I say we had "teamed up", but to tell the truth it was like a race between two bitter rivals: Monty and the American General Patton. Both of them wanted to be the first to reach the city of Messina on Sicily, and be seen as the victor. The trouble with this rivalry between the two generals was that it spread down to the ordinary troops, so that instead of working together as we should have done, just fighting the Germans and Italians, we were encouraged to try and keep one step ahead of the Americans, and Patton encouraged his men to keep one step ahead of us.

In the end the Americans won the race: on 17 August 1943 they entered Messina, and when we arrived they cheered us and called out "Here come the guys who came second!" and "Welcome to the tourists!" Monty was furious; not because of the way the Americans acted towards us but because we British hadn't got to Messina before Patton and the Americans.

In September we moved on to Italy. Again, it was a joint attack with the Americans, but our offensives were concentrated on different parts of the Italian coast. Our target was the Calabria region. Although the Italians surrendered pretty quickly, on 8 September, the German troops in Italy fought so hard that it took the whole winter to defeat them. We suffered a lot of casualties during the Italian campaign, and one of them was Pete. He was shot dead by a sniper while out defusing mines. First Ginger, then Pete. Our gang of four was now down to two – just me and Chalky.

In March 1944, with the battle in Italy still raging, Chalky and I were sent home on leave. Chalky went back to Newcastle to see his folks, and I went home to Camden Town.

It felt strange at home after being away for so long. As I walked along Selous Mews towards our house, my kitbag over my shoulder, our cobbled street seemed so narrow. Even though it was my home, the place where I'd grown up, after all this time away from it, it felt foreign to me. I suppose the desert and the huge amounts of space in North Africa, and the fighting in Sicily and Italy, had changed me.

I knocked on our front door, and when Mum opened it I was shocked to see how tiny and frail she looked.

"So, you've come home, have you?" she said, almost grumpily. It wasn't the welcome I'd expected.

"Yes," I said.

"Make sure you wipe your feet," she told me, stepping back to let me in. "I've just washed the passage."

I felt like a giant in our tiny little house.

"I'll put the kettle on for a cup of tea," said Mum. "Have you eaten?"

"No," I said.

"I'll make you a sandwich," she said. "We're still on rations so I haven't got much. It'll have to be spam."

Spam was a sort of pressed meat that came in tins. It was supposed to be pork, but none of us were ever sure what was really in it. "Spam would be great," I said.

I put my kitbag in the front room and walked into the kitchen, where she already had the kettle on.

"How have you been?" I asked.

"As well as can be expected when there's a war on," she said. "You got through safely, then?"

"Yes," I explained. "I was one of the lucky ones." I thought of Ginger and Pete, and all those thousands of other men who'd gone off to war just like me, and were never coming back but were buried in a grave far from home.

"How are Uncle George and Aunt Ivy?" I asked.

"Your Uncle George is dead," she said, matter-of-factly getting two slices of bread and buttering them for my sandwich.

I stood there, stunned. "Dead?" I echoed.

Mum nodded. "He was out fire-fighting when a bomb hit the building he was trying to save, killing him outright. Ivy's hair turned white overnight when she heard the news, but she's surviving. Nothing else she can do when something like that happens."

Mum finished making the sandwich, put it on a small plate, and placed it in front of me.

"There," she said. "That'll keep you going till supper."

I sat at the kitchen table, looking at the sandwich, and thought about Uncle George and Ginger and Pete, and everyone else I knew who'd died in this war, and suddenly I lost my appetite.

"I'm sorry, Mum," I said. "I'm not hungry."

Mum bridled, upset. "Not hungry?" she said, angrily. "After you've stood there and watched me make it. With food in short supply as well! You eat that sandwich, and be grateful! They may be dead, but the living have to eat. Life goes on."

And so I did. I picked up the sandwich, and did as I was told. It tasted terrible, and it took a lot of chewing, but I ate it. Like Mum said – life goes on.

Epilogue

Chalky and I didn't stay at home on leave long. In June 1944 we were part of the invasion force that landed on the beaches of Normandy. We were both wounded soon after we landed and were invalided back to England. For both of us, that was the end of our war.

After we came out of hospital, Chalky and I kept in touch by letter. He offered to put me up if I visited him, but I was kept busy trying to start up my own business in Uncle George's old garage. Plus I meet a girl and we were talking about getting married. Still, one day me and her will go up north and see Chalky.

Yesterday, 8 May 1945, they told us the War was over. As I heard the news on the radio, I couldn't help but think of all the people I'd known who'd died during the last five and a half years, and I thought: let's hope that something good comes out of this, let's hope that they didn't die in vain.

HISTORICAL NOTE

The battle in North Africa was one of the most crucial in the whole War. In the words of the British Prime Minister at the time, Winston Churchill: "Before Alamein we never had a victory; after Alamein we never had a defeat."

Rommel said later that he believed the destruction of his army in North Africa by Montgomery's Allied troops resulted in Germany losing the War. Rommel believed that if he had been able to get his army back to Italy they could have re-formed.

Astonishingly, neither of the two opposing generals took any part in the opening stages of the Battle of Alamein. On 23 October Rommel was in Austria undergoing medical treatment for blood and liver problems. The entry in Montgomery's diary for that day reads: "In the evening I read a book and went to bed early. At 9.40 pm the barrage of over one thousand guns opened and the Eighth Army went into the attack. At that moment I was asleep in my caravan. There was nothing I could do and I knew I would be needed later."

The "British" Eighth Army in North Africa was not exclusively British. In fact, many of the soldiers in the Eighth

Army came from Australia, New Zealand and South Africa, with units from England, Scotland, India, France and Greece. One third of Rommel's army was made up of Italian soldiers, although his major force was his German Panzer (tank) Divisions.

The destruction of Rommel's army in North Africa meant the way was clear for a combined British-American force to cross the Mediterranean Sea from North Africa to Sicily, and then on to Italy, to force the country to surrender.

The minefields of Alamein

The Battle of Alamein saw some of the largest uses of land mines in the whole of the War. Rommel described the minefields ordered to defend his front-line position as "The Devil's Garden". The largest was five miles deep and had half a million mines laid in two long fields. In the middle of these Rommel positioned anti-tank guns and infantrymen. Rommel believed that The Devil's Garden was impenetrable – that there was no way the British could get through it without suffering so many casualties that the attack would fail.

Because the British were aware of the enormous size of these minefields, and the huge number of deadly mines underfoot (many of them booby-trapped), the opening attack on the night of 23 October was called, with black humour, "Operation Lightfoot".

The attack used both sappers on foot and Scorpion "flail tanks" to try to clear the mines. A lot of the flail tanks broke down and it was left to the sappers to clear the mines by hand. Although many sappers used metal detectors to find mines, most were uncovered by prodding the ground carefully with a bayonet attached to a rifle.

The sappers

The role of the sappers in warfare stretches right back in history: in 52 BC Julius Caesar wrote a detailed account of the military engineering techniques he used in his war in Gaul. He ordered his soldiers to dig long trenches as a defence against the attacking Gauls, and into these trenches he had iron hooks and sharpened stakes fixed, hidden beneath twigs and brushwood.

The sappers have used the same basic system ever since: dig defensive trenches and fill them with objects that will slow down an enemy attack: in modern warfare, these are usually land mines, although in Vietnam in the 1960s and 1970s, the Viet Cong dug deep trenches with sharpened bamboo stakes, some with poisoned tips, as traps for American infantrymen.

Land mines

The earliest exploding land mines, which used gunpowder, first appeared around 1530 in southern Italy. They were called "fougasses". They were actually cannons placed underground and covered with small rocks and debris. A long trail of gunpowder was placed over the ground from the hidden underground cannon to a hiding place, from where – once the attackers were seen approaching – the cannon was set off by igniting the trail of gunpowder. The problem with this method was that gunpowder absorbs water from the air and loses its explosiveness. This meant that the trail of gunpowder could only be laid shortly before the cannon was fired.

Major changes in land mine technology occurred during the American Civil War (1861–65), and they were particularly used by the southern Confederate side. Electrical firing mechanisms were introduced, which meant the mines could be detonated from a distance without the need for gunpowder trails. The pressure-mine also came into operation during the American Civil War. This was partly buried beneath the surface and was detonated by someone stepping on to it and triggering an electrical charge, or simply by breaking a glass container which made a chemical connection, setting off the gunpowder.

During the wars of the twentieth century the use of land mines, particularly those intended to injure or kill an individual, was widespread, with technology becoming evermore sophisticated.

By the end of the twentieth century the human cost

among civilians as a result of land mines – with many hundreds of thousands of people killed or maimed – made some nations realize that the use of land mines had got out of hand. For example, after the first Gulf War many land mines were left in place, and by 1993 1,700 civilians had been killed by them, with many more badly injured. It was calculated that in 1994 there were at least ten million active land mines left in the ground in Afghanistan.

The result was an attempt to control the use of land mines, and also carry out Land mine Clearance Programmes to remove mines left in place after the end of a war. In December 1997 in Ottawa, Canada, an international treaty to ban anti-personnel land mines was signed by 121 nations.

TIMELINE

1 September 1939 Germany invades Poland in defiance of Allies.

3 September 1939 Britain, France, Australia and New Zealand declare war on Germany.

13 September 1940 Italians advance into Egypt.

December 1940 British counter-attack in Egypt.

7 February 1941 Italian forces surrender.

12 February 1941 Rommel takes over Axis forces in North Africa. Launches offensive.

November–December 1941 Operation Crusader by Allies forces Rommel back.

7 December 1941 Japanese attack US fleet at Pearl Harbor, Hawaii.

8 December 1941 USA enters the War.

May–June 1942 Rommel's counter-attack forces Allied retreat.

23 June 1942 German forces cross into Egypt. Allies dig in at El Alamein.

August 1942 Field Marshal Alexander made Commander-in-Chief of Allied forces in Middle East. Montgomery takes over command of Eighth Army.

31 August–6 September 1942 Battle of Alam Halfa: Rommel launches attack.

31 October–4 November 1942 Battle of Alamein. Allied victory.

November 1942 Operation Torch: combined British-American landings in North-West Africa.

March 1943 Rommel leaves North Africa for Europe.

12 May 1943 Remnants of Rommel's army surrenders. War in North Africa ends.

July–September 1943 Allied invasion of Italy. Italy surrenders.

6 June 1944 D-Day: Allies land on Normandy beaches **20 July 1944** Attempt on Hitler's life by German generals fails. Many German officials arrested by Gestapo.

14 October 1944 Rommel, suspected of being part of German generals anti-Hitler plot, forced to commit suicide by Nazi SS.

30 April 1945 Hitler commits suicide.

7 May 1945 Unconditional surrender of German forces.

2 September 1945 Formal surrender of Japan.

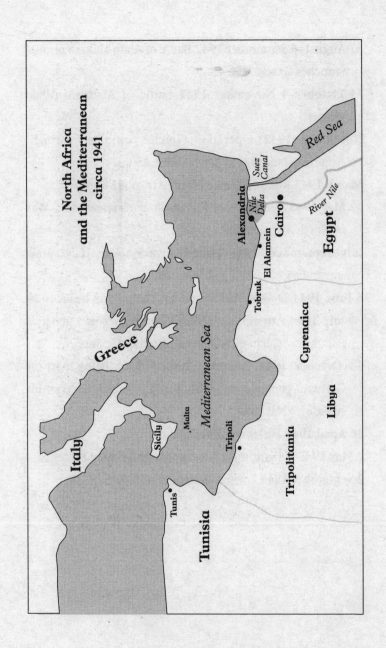

North Africa
and the Mediterranean
circa 1941

Red Sea

Suez Canal

Alexandria
Nile Delta

River Nile

Cairo

Egypt

El Alamein

Tobruk

Cyrenaica

Greece

Mediterranean Sea

Libya

Malta

Italy

Tripoli

Tripolitania

Sicily

Tunis

Tunisia

Rommel, Commander of the Afrika Korps, and nicknamed the "Desert Fox", consults battle plans with his staff.

Field Marshall Montgomery, Commander of the Allied Eighth Army, welcomes Winston Churchill to Tripoli, Libya, in February 1943.

Allied sappers use mine detectors to locate mines on the desert track.

An allied sapper lays a mine in the desert near El Alamein

PICTURE ACKNOWLEDGEMENTS

P138   Map of North Africa and the Mediterranean, Michelle Strong
P139   Rommel and his plans © Mary Evans Picture Library
P140   Montgomery and Churchill © British Pathe – ITN Archive
P141   Allied Sappers © British Pathe – ITN Archive
P142   A Sapper lays a land mine © British Pathe – ITN Archive